Cottage

Cottage

America's Favorite Home Inside and Out

M. CAREN CONNOLLY
AND LOUIS WASSERMAN

The Taunton Press

The Taunton Press
Inspiration for hands-on living®

The Taunton Press, Inc., 63 South Main Street, PO Box 5506, Newtown, CT 06470-5506
e-mail: tp@taunton.com

Editors: Wendy Jordan, Peter Chapman
Jacket/Cover design: Alexander Isley Inc.
Interior design and layout: Susan Fazekas
Illustrator: Louis Wasserman
Photographer: Rob Karosis

LIBRARY OF CONGRESS CATALOGING-IN-PUBLICATION DATA
Connolly, M. Caren.
  Cottage : America's favorite home inside and out / M. Caren Connolly and Louis Wasserman.
    p. cm.
  ISBN 1-56158-731-1
  1. Cottages--United States. 2. Country homes--United States. I. Wasserman, Louis. II. Title.
  NA7561.C655 2005
  728'.37'0973--dc22
                        2005002923

Printed in Singapore
10 9 8 7 6 5 4 3 2 1

To our friends,
who always encourage us to take on a challenge and
then help us meet it with wisdom and laughter

ACKNOWLEDGMENTS

This book represents our third joint endeavor with the creative team at
The Taunton Press. We don't know how Taunton does it, but it keeps
adding the best and the brightest while retaining its all-star staff members.
To our trusted teammates, we owe our thanks. Peter Chapman personifies grace
under pressure. With steady composure he kept a firm hand on the editorial
compass of this book. Paula Schlosser is to be congratulated for once again mak
ing elegance look easy. Thank you to Maria Taylor, Carol Singer, Wendi Mijal, and
Robyn Aitken for all their behind-the-scenes work. And a sincere thank you to
publisher Jim Childs for this third opportunity and to Steve Culpepper for his
early support. Without the art of photographers Rob Karosis, Ken Gutmaker,
and Mark Samu the book just wouldn't be as good as it is. Allison Hollett and
her marketing staff continue to work their wonders.

Thanks go out as well to our new teammates—Maureen Graney who got
the ball rolling, and Katie Benoit who kept it moving. Without Wendy Jordan's
gentle, but persistent, editorial guidance this book might still be rounding
the bases.

A heartfelt thank you to all the owners of the cottages in the book, gracious
folks who allowed us to share with you a glimpse into their most intimate
homes. And thanks to the architects and designers who understand so well what
makes a cottage a cottage.

CONTENTS

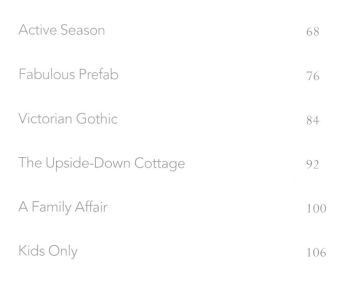

The Cottage Connection

Cottages are all about connections—connections between the natural and built environment, between indoor and outdoor living, and between tradition and innovation in construction. In a time when it is common for family members to live in different parts of the country, if not in different parts of the world, a cottage can also be the family connection, everyone's favorite home. Cottages are homes where memories are as strong a foundation as bricks and mortar. They often are built as legacies, connections with future generations.

Cottage experiences are highly individual. When Louis was growing up in Wisconsin, the word *cottage* was synonymous with vacations "Up North." Many summers, his family and a group of friends rented neighboring cottages. They fished during the day and played cards at night. Over the years all the summers have melded together into one delightful, seamless memory. For a time, Caren and her family of six lived in a stone cottage with a thatched roof and a pink Dutch door in the thick pinewoods of Carmel, California. The cottage was so tiny that her brother slept in a closet. But for a small girl, living in the little cottage was like living in a fairytale.

For many people, cottage living is a dream come true. And, as the cottages in our book show, every dream is different. Cottage owners typically ignore the commonly accepted real estate maxims, such as building for resale, maximizing square footage, including a bathroom for every bedroom, and tacking on a three-car garage. Instead they think outside the box and create intimate homes that express their personalities and how they enjoy living their lives. The cottages in this book, and the dreams of their owners, have cast a spell over us. We invite you to read their stories and imagine yourself enjoying the hospitality each cottage graciously offers.

At Home

When cottage owners describe their homes, they speak more of mood than of mortar. Ask them about their cottage and a faraway look comes into their eyes, as if they have already begun the journey to their ideal getaway. Cottage living heightens awareness of the sensual qualities of the landscape—the sweetness of the mountain air, the sound of pine needles crunching underfoot, the feel of walking on the sandy beach, the taste of the salt air. And anticipation—those thoughts of the cottage, its natural setting and its simple, refreshing lifestyle—is an important part of the cottage experience inside and out.

There's something lyrical about cottages, something that strikes a deep chord. Whether large or small, plain or ornate, full-time residences or vacation destinations, cottages ring true to the image of America's favorite homes—one-of-a-kind designs that are in tune with nature.

◁ The handrail adds a new twist to a winding stair as it welcomes cottage dwellers and visitors to a new chapter in cottage living.

△ Cottage owners tend to select building materials that favor the local landscape and climate. This delightful standing-seam, metal-roofed wood and stone cottage is a natural fit to rainy, forested Seattle.

What Makes a Cottage a Cottage?

Of all the different types of homes, cottages may be the most difficult to pin down with a precise definition. Colonials, Cape Cods, bungalows, and ranches all have strict design criteria that prescribe their pedigree. Cottages are more intuitive; woven into the fabric of every culture's folk tales, they represent the universal home. They are best defined by look and feel rather than by architectural rules. Built in every style imaginable, from High Victorian to high-tech, cottages come in every size as well. Some contemporary cottages can easily pass for mansions, just like the 1890s "cottages" of Newport, Rhode Island, and Jeykll Island, Georgia. Others are almost as tiny as Thomas Jefferson's two-room honeymoon cottage at Monticello. The cottages featured in this book range in size from 400 sq. ft.

▷ Open windows and randomly spaced board sheathing don't pose energy-loss concerns for this uninsulated, summer-only cottage. Honest and humble, the materials add to the rustic charm of this 1890s cottage.

▷ The all-white color scheme is a traditional choice for southern cottages. Light colors reflect the heat and have a clean, crisp look that's welcome in a warm climate. The brick piers lift the cottage off the ground, another traditional cooling technique.

to 3,200 sq. ft., and from one-room shelters to quilts of cozy rooms. If it is neither style nor size that prescribes a cottage, you may ask, "What makes a cottage a cottage?" We define a cottage as a home that is intimate, bucolic, and quintessentially expressive of the owner's imagination.

Cottages are charismatic homes that have the gift of conveying the unique imprint of their owners' personalities, through renovation, addition, or new construction. This book has widely diverse examples. There's the transformation of a rundown 1920s Seattle worker's cottage into a contemporary, colorful, and kid-filled family home. And a brand new North Carolina fishing retreat that looks as though it has always been at the base of its mountain. Simultaneously, cottages communicate affection for their settings and enthusiasm for local building traditions and materials, as shown by

△ **This prefab cottage was designed to be adaptable to a wide range of landscapes, from flat plains to rolling hills; it recalls the angular forms of agricultural buildings that fit so comfortably in rural areas.**

COTTAGE PEDIGREE

THE GOLDEN AGE OF COTTAGES

The 1890s are often referred to as the golden age of cottage architecture. City living was considered unhealthy back then, and a summer trip to the mountains or the shore to take in the fresh air was regarded as the antidote. Affordable and convenient, the newly expanded rail and steamboat transportation systems made these out-of-the-way destinations much more accessible, and construction of summer cottages flourished. Built with indigenous materials and following vernacular building traditions, these simple cottages expressed a close connection to their location.

Airy Steamboat Gothic summer cottages, seemingly all porch and window, were embellished with fancy scrollsaw woodwork reminiscent of the steamboats that brought vacationers to their waterfront cottages. The ornamented

Victorian, gracious Shingle, and moody Gothic styles feel at home at both wooded and shore sites.

Because summer living was focused on outdoor activities, cottage interiors were intentionally informal and communal. White painted beaded board, plain wood floors, and dormitory style bedrooms with iron bedsteads were the norm. Generous porches encouraged casual gatherings in the fresh air.

In the past 200 years, not too much about cottage design has changed. The artful craftsmanship and cozy floor plans of the 19th-century cottage genre remain very appealing. Cottage craftsmen continue to employ local and traditional construction methods and indigenous materials. And vernacular variations on classic architectural styles still clearly express regional differences.

△ Tactile and ornamented, cottage exteriors have a strong visual connection to their surroundings. Rather than dominate, they fit gracefully into their particular site.

△ This former worker's cottage needed more than a facelift: it required a new foundation, three additional bedrooms, a bath, and a garage. But at 1,870 sq. ft., the remodeled cottage is still considerably smaller than the average subdivision home.

the conversion of two historic structures—a barn in Pennsylvania and a one-room schoolhouse in Missouri —into weekend retreats. As wide-ranging as they are in style, cottages share a set of exterior and interior characteristics that bring into being that ineffable cottage charm.

Cottage Exteriors

A beguiling aspect of cottage homes is the unique and serendipitous way in which built and natural features form a web that cannot be disentangled. And while *unique* and *serendipitous* are two indisputable cottage adjectives, these homes do have certain exterior characteristics in common: a reliance on nature for the aesthetic concept, respect for tradition in form and craft, and a seamless connection between outdoor rooms and the natural surroundings.

At One with Nature

Whether a cottage lies on a Florida beach or is hidden deep within the Michigan woods, the natural setting, locally available building materials, regional building traditions, and views all play a major role in determining what the cottage

At one with nature
- Rough wood siding
- Stone path and walls
- Windows connect to outdoors
- Graceful fit with site

Respect for tradition
- Board and batten siding
- Simple window trim
- Metal roofing

Seamless inside-outside connection
- Outdoor rooms
- Visual connection to outdoor amenity

exterior looks like. Contemporary Florida beach cottages have deep roof overhangs that provide shade and light-colored metal roofs that reflect the heat. Generous, shady second-story porches are great places to revel in views of water and sunset while enjoying cooling breezes. At the other extreme, cottages in the northern woods tend to be low, introverted, mysterious homes that blend into dense forests under the cover of the tree canopy.

Cottage form is often influenced by traditional construction methods used in vernacular structures that predate contemporary heating and cooling systems. Historic barns and houses provide cues to cottage designers for the best orientation and forms to maximize the positive benefits of ventilation, sunlight, and shade.

△ Bank barns, typical of the Pennsylvania barn building tradition, often have stone bases to wick moisture away from the wood siding. These original "split levels" provide easy indoor-outdoor access for sites with noticeable grade change.

△ Cottages are homes where outdoor rooms are integrated into the floor plan and are enjoyed as fully as indoor rooms.

△ The grassy lawn preserves the look of an 1850s country schoolyard. The stone chimney has a warm, substantial presence on the side of the house but, since the original building did not have a fireplace, the architects made sure it would not dominate the view from the approach drive.

Exteriors constructed of natural materials, such as stone and wood, age gracefully, mellowing over time and acquiring a rich natural patina from the weathering effects of sun, wind, rain, and snow. New cottages, built with materials characteristic of their region, stand out as singular precisely because they harmonize in color, material, texture, and scale with their natural surroundings.

Cottages are meant to be touched; their forms, materials, and details immediately connect us to nature's tactile qualities. Wood siding may be rough-sawn rather than smooth; the joints are emphasized with V grooves or battens that have a strong dimensional quality. Stone foundations and base courses, whether craggy or worn, have an unmistakable feel and heft. Mossy, upturned wood shakes and smooth standing-seam metal add textural appeal to the traditional steeply pitched cottage roof.

RESPECT FOR TRADITION

Many new cottages revive Gothic, Shingle style, and other picturesque styles, which are synonymous with the romantic ideal of living close to nature. Other cottages celebrate the ethnic heritage of their owners or the region. From the Swedish-style cottage in Washington State to the dogtrot cottage in northern California and the Bahamian-inspired beach cottage in Florida, the examples in this book express a plethora of ethnic and vernacular traditions.

Local craftsmen are a boon when it comes to replicating highly crafted special touches that give a cottage its one-of-a-kind appeal. They bring with them the knowledge of local history, vernacular architecture, and construction methods handed down from an earlier generation of immigrant craftsmen who built the now historic structures. A new stone cottage in Tennessee is the beneficiary of skills handed down by Irish stonemasons who built roads and bridges across the state in the 1800s. The richly ornamented wood cottages of the North Central and Southern states continue the legacy of carpenters and furniture makers who lived and worked in these heavily wooded regions.

New cottages are borrowing a page from an old book when it comes to designing sustainable homes that live lightly on the land. At one end of the spectrum is the new interest in prefabricated structures that are factory built and assembled on site, like the Aperture House in Wisconsin. And at the other end is the California straw bale house, hand-constructed on site by the owners and their friends.

SEAMLESS CONNECTION TO THE OUTDOORS

Many activities connected to the outdoors—boating, swimming, fishing, bird and whale watching, hiking, and active games—are a vital and fun part of cottage life. Taking full advantage of its natural setting, every cottage has a full complement of outdoor rooms, from screened-in sleeping and dining porches to grassy clearings in the woods. Quite often the square footage of these outdoor rooms equals or exceeds the sum total of the square footage of interior rooms. Porches literally give a small cottage extra breathing room, without compromising the intimate scale of the interior. Many cottage owners identify the porch as their favorite place to read, daydream, play cards, and visit with friends.

Doors, from swinging Dutch doors to sliding barn doors, provide a fluid connection between inside and out. Anticipation,

△▷ **The owners of this straw-bale cottage chose the location for its natural beauty. Taking care to preserve the site rather than overwhelm it, they chose native grasses that tolerate the hot summers and dry winters and flourish in the spring rains.**

A Deck by Any Other Name

{ Inside & Out } Every cottage featured in this book has at least one outdoor room. The rooms range from simple to luxurious, and from tiny to square footage that rivals the cottage interior. Because many cottages draw from historical styles, regional architectural traditions, or the owner's cultural traditions, the outdoor rooms vary greatly and have all sorts of names, most of them much more intriguing than today's *porch* and *deck*.

There is the *portico* of the Victorian-style cottage in an Ohio Chautauqua community, the wood *arcade* that leads to a Scandinavian-style woodland cottage in Washington's San Juan islands (shown here), the *veranda* of a Florida beach cottage, and the *dogtrot* between the wings of a California straw-bale cottage. Each outdoor room is different, yet each expresses the cottage owner's idea of an ideal relationship to nature.

adventure, mystery, and surprise are built into the cottage approach. As cottage doors are often configured in multiples to frame particular landscape views, the front door is only one of many. Front doors, grand, boastful icons in many residential neighborhoods, can be downright difficult to find in cottage conclaves.

Other exterior design elements also play an important role in shaping the character of the cottage. Perky roof dormers with odd-sized windows add personality and extra headroom under sloped roofs. They also vent hot air from potentially stuffy second-story rooms. Gable ends, often topped with fanciful finials, provide sufficient height and width for the placement of opposing double-hung or casement windows, thus facilitating cross-ventilation and framing significant views.

Cottage Interiors

Cottage interiors enchantingly incorporate the imagination, emotions, and individuality of the owners in a highly personal manner. Cottages are richly atmospheric, intimate in scale, and unsurpassed in creating harmony between indoor and outdoor spaces.

▷ The large hearthstones are the right scale for the double-height great room fireplace. Salvaged from an old barn, the splintered wood mantelpiece suits the heft and girth of the hearth; the antique tinderbox keeps matches handy.

Personal touches

Intimate scale
• Moldings and details create intimate scale

INSIDE
THE COTTAGE

Indoor-outdoor harmony
• Bringing the outside in
• Natural materials

Creating a mood
• Cottages are...romantic, comfortable, intimate, warm in feeling and in color

CREATING A MOOD

When it comes to cottage interiors, it is accepted that the heart rules the head. Floor plans are intuitive and sometimes unconventional, revolving around views, ventilation, day-light, topography, and lifestyle. Upside-down plans—with bedrooms on the first floor and living rooms above—are perfectly acceptable. Under shady overhangs, first-floor bedrooms are cool and quiet, while social gathering spaces upstairs take advantage of premium views.

At a cottage, tucking children's beds into a dining room alcove is both charming and appropriate. Kitchens are free to take over as much (or as little) square footage as suits the family. Cottage kitchens in this book range from small niches carved out of living rooms to generous rooms at the heart of the home around which activities revolve. How cottage

△ This contemporary cottage makes the most of the island views. The freestanding fireplace, glass-fronted china cabinet, and interior windows create a strong sense of transparency, while the upper floor affords a panoramic view.

▷ "Bigger than it looks" is the ultimate compliment for this 1,450-sq.-ft. cottage. Understanding scale and borrowing views of distant landscapes, the designers have worked their magic to create the illusion of more space.

△ From any vantage point in a cottage the allure of the outdoors is omnipresent. The varied sizes and shapes of the windows and doors in cottages are designed to frame beautiful views, bring in shimmering sunlight, enhance natural ventilation, and facilitate the harmonious flow of activities from indoors to outdoors.

space is used depends entirely on the way the owners want to live and the mood they want to create.

Color schemes express the personalities of the cottage owners, too. The same team of architects designed the two North Carolina Island cottages in this book, yet the palettes are strikingly different. One cottage has a vibrant orange, blue and white interior patterned after the couple's favorite painting; the other is filled with the soft, muted green, gray, and white that the owners love in their beach landscape.

Whimsy and humor are more accepted as design tools in cottages than in more formal residential styles. As cottages are personal places, many of the jokes are private and can be appreciated fully only by the owners and close friends. Witty cottage names, such as Katzablanca, bring smiles year after year.

INTIMATE SCALE

While newly constructed cottages have done away with noggin-bashing beams and low ceilings, cottages still are designed, inside and out, at the scale of the human hand and body. Looking at every square inch with an innovative eye (or a gimlet wink) is a cottage design tradition. The varying scale of rooms, from expansive shared spaces to tiny nooks and crannies, lends a convivial feel to cottage living. No cottage would be complete without a collection of quirky spaces—cozy lofts sized just right for children to while away a rainy afternoon, oversized porches, and novel cubbies for storing wine or towels.

Knowing when to exaggerate and when to understate is key to creating just the right cottage scale. As Rob Whitten's design for a double-height living room illustrates, cottages effectively use the illusion of grandeur rather than wasted square footage to create drama. On the other hand, large rooms can appear far more intimate when they are tucked under sloping ceiling planes punctuated with eccentric window sizes and shapes, as in the home office in Garry and Nancy's Connecticut cottage.

Don't be fooled by the simple cottage interiors. Dozens of small decisions, such as how many mullions to use in the windows, what width to make the handrail, or how wide the floor planks should be, need to be answered in concert to produce the winning combination of scale and detail that makes cottages feel "just right."

Indoor-Outdoor Harmony

Interior finishes, like cottage exteriors, are tactile and expressive. Cottage designers strive to use local natural materials such as stone and wood in both structural and aesthetic ways to make the connection to the outside as transparent as possible. Granite beach stones gathered by the owners face a Connecticut fireplace; weathered barn siding is recycled in North Carolina and Pennsylvania cottages; and iron accents pay homage to the rich ore deposits of the northern Midwest. Exposed logs, timber columns, rough-hewn beams, and naturally finished wood panels are perennially favored as finish materials.

Most cottages use local materials on the interior that convey a strong connection with the immediate surroundings. Wood flooring, for example, often comes from trees grown in local tree farms. Highly varnished yellow pine floors are a natural choice in Georgia or Florida. The smooth red tones of Douglas fir are found in the cottages in the Pacific Northwest.

◁ Flexible sleeping arrangements are a necessary ingredient for carefree hospitality. Small, individual windows in each bunk create a roomlike feel.

△ A carefully considered lighting plan sets the stage for a romantic cottage atmosphere. This combination of spot and pendant lights glamorizes the sculptural volumes of the vaulted ceiling while efficiently lighting the kitchen work surfaces.

▷ This new cottage incorporates luxury in its first-floor en suite bathrooms. The dressing room with double sinks leads into the tiled bathing room, with a private water closet beyond.

▽ There isn't a bad seat in the cottage. With three-quarters of the second-floor perimeter glazed, all the guests enjoy a view while dining. Fittingly, the cook has the best view of all.

Fast-growing wetland trees such as poplar create a surprisingly sophisticated pale and elegant wood for flooring in low-lying coastal areas. Floors of woodland cottages reflect the varied tones of white or red oak.

Enjoying the Company of Family and Friends

Most 19th- and early 20th-century American cottages were rustic, seasonal, and bucolic getaways. The first week of a cottage visit was often spent priming the pump, cleaning out bird and mouse nests, and scrubbing up mildew to get the cottage ready for occupancy. Today, expectations are far different. Cottage owners dream about flexible, intimately scaled, well-designed homes that are low-maintenance, ready to enjoy, and built to last for many years. Most owners want to spend as much time as possible at their cottages, using them on weekends, for vacations and, increasingly, even as full-time residences.

Enjoying the company of friends and family in an idyllic setting is a true pleasure of cottage living. Deciding where to put all the guests and how to feed them brings out creative and flexible solutions. Window seats become guest beds at night, and hallways and back porches frequently are converted into guest bedrooms. Flexible arrangement of furniture transforms porches into dining rooms. The magical cottage scale ensures that whether two people or 12 are visiting, everyone is cozy and comfortable.

There are circumstances when incorporating enough bedrooms, baths, stairs and circulation space to accommodate large numbers of visitors can jeopardize the intimate scale of a cottage and alter the character of the landscape. Owners of several cottages in this book found that building a simple guest cottage a short distance away is a delightful way to maintain family privacy

and provide hospitality. When not occupied by guests, the little cottages often are enjoyed as studios or away space for family members.

With family members and guests coming from many different directions, it is not unusual for cottage owners to add a two or even three-car garage to their house. Typically the garage is placed some distance away so that its boxy, utilitarian form does not detract from the intimate scale of the cottage. That separation is part of the cottage lifestyle; after all, dodging raindrops with an armful of groceries is a natural part of indoor outdoor living. Garages also provide much-needed secure storage and work space for hobbies, without claiming square feet from the cottage proper.

Building New Traditions

New cottages, like old cottages, respond to dreams. A new generation of Americans is continuing the tradition of living in homes that express their own personalities and their attitude toward nature. While scale, texture, and connection to nature are timeless ingredients of successful cottage design, today's cottage owners (and designers) are breaking through the tethers of strict historical reconstruction to cast cottages in a more contemporary light.

The new-generation cottage may look old, but be built using radically new technology. A Victorian-style cottage, for example, may be built to current "healthy house" standards. Another may look strikingly contemporary and be built with low-tech straw bale construction. In the spirit of American ingenuity, we are continually reinventing cottages. We love to build on tradition, introducing a twist that marks cottages as our own. It's our way of continuing the legacy of the cottage as America's favorite home.

△ A front porch is the perfect place to start a cottage conversation. Comfortable chairs invite folks to slow down and enjoy the intricate details crafted by generations of deft craftsmen.

The Cottages

One Plus One
Equals One

Neither retreat nor vacation home, this tiny cottage on the edge of Puget Sound is enjoyed as often as a busy work schedule allows. When the owner bought the property, she asked architect Ross Chapin to design a cottage for the site that would require removing as few trees as possible. Because a small building is easiest to fit between trees, Ross proposed that they construct two small cottages—an intimate main cottage and a 220-sq.-ft. guest cottage 20 ft. away. The two-story, one-bedroom, one-bath main cottage is smaller than most urban apartments, but the gorgeous setting and expansive views endow it with a generous and luxurious feel.

One-of-a-Kind Houses

One hallmark that sets cottages apart is that each is one of a kind, and cottage owners revel in this uniqueness. Designs for most cottages come from the owner's heart, not from thoughts about resale. The owner of this cottage wanted the first-floor living/dining alcove and kitchen to flow together. She requested one large second-floor bedroom where she could enjoy whale watching and eagle watching from the

◁ **Chosen with care to capture the view and to adhere to Washington State's well thought out energy code, the boldly banded windows give the cottage a wide-eyed, cheerful demeanor.**

▷ **Overnight guests enjoy the intimate scale and privacy of the adjacent studio/guest cottage. Wide window trim, corner boards, fascia, frieze, and belly-band, all painted white, give the small structure the appearance of a dollhouse.**

comfort of an easy chair. Storage was a high priority, too; the combination of a second-floor dressing room and first-floor storage room provides more stowing space than the owner ever imagined possible in such a small cottage.

Rather than devoting square footage to a second bedroom that would be used only occasionally, Ross made the second-floor hallway just a little wider than the standard dimension. The well-lit "hallroom," as the owner calls it, accommodates bookshelves and a work and hobby desk. In a nook at the head of the open staircase are built-in drawers with a daybed on top that doubles as an overnight spot for close friends or family.

The See-Through House

Windows are an important feature in cottage design. Ross employs three different window styles here: tall two-over-two corner windows; narrower and shorter windows in the

▷ **Highly varnished knotty pine enfolds the dining alcove. The deep banquette is multipurpose: The benches are built-in storage units with wide backs that work as shelves, and the sills are wide enough to hold coffee cups.**

NEW NOOK
OF THE NORTH

{Nooks & Crannies} Sometimes the best design decisions are right in front of your eyes. By making a corridor 2 ft. wider and colonizing the headroom space above the stair, Ross Chapin has created a study and office area complete with daybed. Everything has been thought out so well that each element does double duty. The daybed serves as couch by day and visitor's bed by night, while providing storage around the clock. The corridor double-dips as work area and circulation space to bed and bath.

△ The tiled-topped backsplash provides extra counter space and hides cooking operations from the entry and the living room. The tiny 9-ft. by 9-ft. kitchen and dining nook is the activity hub of this intimately scaled cottage.

▷ In some cultures, red signifies happiness and prosperity. The red gate and door are cheery guides, leading visitors like gay beacons to the gray cottages that huddle in the shadows of surrounding trees.

△ Pairing two windows at the corners presents a panoramic view of the landscape from the living room and kitchen. Slender white mullions set into the tall rectangular windows dissolve into the glass.

{ Inside & Out } Windows are like a building's eyes upon the world. What better way to get a feel for a cottage's personality than to look into its windows?

Inside the cottage, window placement must complement interior function, take advantage of views, respond to solar orientation, and provide necessary ventilation. Placement in the exterior wall raises the level of complexity because windows in different rooms with different needs and functions must come together in a composition that works visually.

If windows are the eyes of a cottage, the elevation is its face. Cottage elevations are about many design elements—windows, proportion, color, texture, function, and shape—all working together to make a pleasing mix. From the exterior the windows of this cottage are unified by the consistent trim and the masterful, often symmetrical window placement. Whether small vignettes or extra-large casements masquerading as double-hungs, the windows look toward the great view. All these different windows are brought together by their uniform molding size to make a comfortable elevation and a cozy design.

same two-over-two pattern in the hallway, dining nook, and kitchen; and square portholes that frame small vignette views of the sky and treetops. The simple formula creates harmonious variety. As the glazing is reduced in scale, the exterior trim and millwork proportionately expand for a hefty look that contrasts nicely with the light effect of the corner windows.

Stacked over each other in the living room and bedroom, the double corner windows afford wide-angle views out to the surrounding landscape. And from the exterior, the windows make the cottage corners visually dissolve, allowing you to see all the way through the cottage to the trees and water beyond.

Opposites Attract

Applying basic color theory can literally add dimension to a cottage. While the white exterior trim of the windows, corner boards, water table, fascia, and rafters gives the cottage an airy look, the cranberry red doors add weight and depth. That's because red is the opposite of green on the color wheel, so that when the two colors are in close proximity,

◁ Varying the scale of materials gives clues to the hierarchy of spaces and their functions. Heavy brackets trumpet this entrance, and wide clapboard siding distinguishes the main cottage from the storage lean-to, with its narrower shiplap siding.

FIRST FLOOR

Kitchen

Living room

Storage

Covered porch

Eating alcove

SECOND FLOOR

Bath

Closet

Bedroom

Daybed

Desk

▽ The standing-seam metal roof extends over the porch like a warmhearted handshake, welcoming friends even before they enter the cottage. Generous windows and French doors offer glimpses of the bright and casual interior.

△ The shiny finish of the knotty pine walls and ceiling in the woodsy guest cottage projects a clean, crisp, rustic look that matches the character and tone of the dining nook in the main cottage.

△ Silky-smooth blond floorboards, honey-pine door molding, dark-stained porch decking, and white-painted wood trellis highlight the delightfully diverse possibilities for wood finishes. Fittingly, the shaggy fir tree trunk looks just like a porch column.

the eye perceives red as advancing and green as receding. The result is an illusion of added depth. As a subliminal bonus, a red door looks weightier and more secure than a white door.

Both the interior and exterior rely on a color palette drawn from the cottage's natural surroundings. The green siding blends in with the evergreen boughs that shelter the cottage. The white trim, gray metal roof, and red door reflect cool colors found in the landscape. On the interior, the warm pine walls, ceiling decking, window and door trim, and the oak floors are naturally finished to highlight the variation in color and texture of the fir, pine, and hemlock woods. With the exception of the terra-cotta walls of the snug dining nook, all the painted walls are the same soft fawn color. The use of one dominant color with one or two accent colors ties the rooms together visually, something important to remember when your cottage is just a little more than 1,000 sq. ft.

To Your Health

P at and Patti's love affair with the historic Chautauqua town of Lakeside, Ohio, on the shores of Lake Erie, began 20 years ago when they stopped there for lunch at a tearoom en route to Toledo. On their return, they stayed one night in the 1875 Victorian hotel in town. For the next two decades, they spent their summers at Lakeside, living in rental houses but always on the lookout for the perfect Victorian cottage to buy. Eventually, they bought a double lot four blocks from the lake and hired an architect and builder to design and build a two-story cottage specifically to their requirements. The architect they chose was Robert Bruce, whose reputation is borne out by the 30-plus cottages he has designed in Lakeside.

Some of the cottages in Lakeside are 130 years old, and many of the new cottages are built in the Victorian style. The couple wanted their cottage to fit the historical nature of the community, accommodate their hobbies—quilting, pottery, and collecting Depression glass—and be a comfortable place for their children and grandchildren to gather. Also, because Pat and Patti have allergies that are aggravated by indoor air pollution, they needed a "healthy house."

◁ A fan is tucked into the exposed structure of the 10-ft.-high porch ceiling to stir the air on still and humid summer nights. The 10-ft. depth of the porch allows for flexible furniture groupings.

29

Healthy Mind, Healthy Body

Healthy-house construction methods and materials differ from those used in conventional construction. Rather than chemically treated wood members, light-gauge metal was used for the floors, walls, and roof framing. Special ventilation and filtration systems—including air changes, filter types, and equipment—were also used. These healthy-house systems are largely invisible, though. With its colorful trim moldings, porch rails, and lap siding, the cottage still fits right into the community of stick-built Victorian cottages. When guests enter the cottage, they find an atmosphere of old-fashioned hospitality rather than space-age technology.

Three generations of family enjoy spending summers at the cottage. The child-friendly community gives the grandchildren freedom to explore and renew summer friendships. The children love walking to the beach, the toy shop, and the ice cream store, and the whole family often uses golf carts or bicycles instead of cars to go from place to place. Tucked under the sundeck is a storage shed that has 14-ft.-high ceilings, tall enough to hang all the bicycles and strollers on wall hooks between visits.

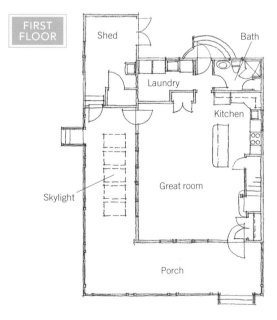

△ Varying finishes is a simple and subtle way to add visual punch to an interior. Here, the kitchen cabinets and wall trim are treated with a matte finish, while the floor and newel post have a high-gloss seal.

LAKESIDE CHAUTAUQUA

At a time just after the Civil War, when there was little organized adult education in America, Lewis Miller and Rev. John Vincent founded an institute at Lake Chautauqua in New York State to provide adult education and training for Sunday school teachers.

Held in an outdoor setting during the summer, the first assembly in 1874 drew a throng of 12,000 people. At the second "Chautauqua" meeting the next summer, President Ulysses S. Grant addressed 60,000 attendees from the porch of Rev. Vincent's cottage, which had been prefabricated in Akron, Ohio, and shipped by train and steamship to the lakefront site. Although Methodist in its underpinnings, the Chautauqua as a general forum for adult education quickly took hold. By 1880, millions of Americans were learning about the arts and religion at Chautauquas around the country.

At the original Chautauqua location, 480 cottages had been built by 1878. Soon cottages sprang up in Oak Bluffs, Massachusetts, Bay View, Michigan, Lakeside, Ohio, and more than 32 other popular Chautauqua locations as well. Summer tent platforms served as the foundations for these minimal cottages, which had no insulation, kitchens, or bathrooms. (Communal dining, education, and bathing facilities were provided for the assembled crowds at large "greens.") Floor plans were replicated, with only gingerbread ornamentation and paint schemes to distinguish one Victorian cottage from another. Mark Twain quipped, "Partitions were so thin that you could hear the women changing their minds."

The porch is an archetypal cottage element that says welcome and provides shelter. This comfortable outdoor room is spacious enough for several people to gather for conversation or a meal.

▷ Outdoor dining is a real treat, especially after spending the winter months indoors. The waterproof iron and glass table is a natural for porch use. The rope chairs dry quickly and provide cool seating on hot days.

▽ Wraparound porches make great exterior rooms, but sometimes they block light to interior rooms. Multiple skylights on the porch and clerestory windows along the wall bring light into the great room.

The free-flowing, open-plan living rooms and wraparound porch of the 1,650-sq.-ft, three-bedroom cottage offer the right mix of variety and togetherness for dynamic family gatherings. The porch is one of the family's favorite places to sit and swing, tell stories, read books, and share meals, even on cool or rainy days. On the second floor, Pat and Patti have a sundeck off their master bedroom where they like to sit after dinner for dessert and conversation. The cottage is built on a steep hill and the first floor has 10-ft.-high ceilings, giving the sundeck a high perch and great views of the Fourth of July fireworks and sunrises over Lake Erie.

Healthy and Sustainable

{ Inside & Out } To ensure that this would be an energy-conserving as well as a healthy house, the architect wrote sustainable requirements into the contract documents, complete with specifications and recommended reading for the contractor. One of the major resources was the U.S. Green Building Council, a leader in the sustainable house movement. Over the last 10 years, the council has continued to refine its Leadership in Energy and Environmental Design (LEED) rating system to evaluate plans and buildings and consequently advance healthy, sustainable construction.

Behind its traditional facade, this cottage features a sustainable, environmentally friendly structure composed of light-gauge steel framing, most of which has been recycled. The construction materials chosen for the house emit minimal VOCs, or volatile organic compounds, the dangerous gases that are released by many building products. Even the traditional wood floors rate highly by LEED standards because they are renewable materials and, being dust-free, minimize allergic reactions. The house was carefully sealed to reduce the intrusion of toxins and pollutants, while retaining the conditioned interior air for allergy control and energy conservation.

◁ **Doubling and tripling columns of the same size is a great way to add visual interest and strength to porch corners and openings. The spaces between the columns allow light in and views out.**

▷ **Cottages often contain surprises. A queen-sized Murphy bed is hidden behind these quilt-worker's curtains, making it easy to convert the sewing room into an extra guest room.**

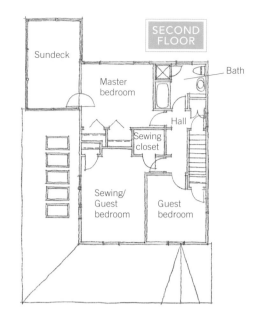

SECOND FLOOR

Sundeck

Master bedroom

Bath

Hall

Sewing closet

Sewing/ Guest bedroom

Guest bedroom

Clean, Crisp, Light, and Bright

Pat and Patti had fun planning and decorating their special place. To settle on an exterior color scheme, they studied photographs of polychrome Victorian houses, known as Painted Ladies, and met with a color consultant. Because they wanted the cottage exterior to reflect colors in the landscape, they picked five main colors—all muted, natural tones—plus two additional crisp hues for the porch ceiling and floors.

Patti is a quilter and Pat is a potter. Patti's clean, crisp, light, and bright quilt designs inspired the interior design of the cottage. The bright white walls are just right to showcase Patti's work and highlight Pat's pottery and their Depression-era glass collection. Patti's sewing room easily converts to a guest room; a large sewing closet ensures that projects in progress are not disturbed. All-white furniture is used throughout the house and on the porch. Some of the wicker furniture is antique, and all of it fits the casual, comfortable look and indoor-outdoor lifestyle the couple likes.

The solid maple kitchen cabinets were finished with a white semitransparent stain, or pickled, for a light, healthy-house finish that is easier to maintain than paint. The floors throughout the house are white birch, with the exception of ceramic in the two bathrooms and the laundry room.

The cottage is about an hour's drive from Pat and Patti's year-round home, so it is easy for them to drive out for some R and R. Patti feels that life at the cottage stimulates her creativity. And she's glad that Pat can stay in Lakeside all weekend and still make it to work on time on Monday mornings, energized by his cottage getaway.

△ Towel rods fill a wall recess outside the bathroom. Tall people use the upper towels, and smaller people the lower ones. The towel wall is an efficient and decorative use of space

◁ Good cottage design simplifies life for the cottage dwellers. Easily accessed extra storage is provided under the stair, discreetly camouflaged behind an angled-top beaded-board door.

Hiding in Plain Sight

James and Diane's cottage is nestled in a high forest hollow not far from Tennessee's largest wildlife preserve. Summer visitors have been flocking to this Cumberland Plateau area since the 1850s when the advent of the railroad allowed families to flee the humid lowlands to heights above the Sewanee River, once nicknamed the "Malaria Line." No longer remote, the area is now only a short commute from Nashville and Chattanooga. But the high elevation and fresh, forest breezes still make it seem a world away.

Privacy is a key component of cottage living, and sometimes the best way to achieve privacy is to hide a cottage in plain sight. To avoid calling attention to this 1,950-sq.-ft. cottage, Bauer Askew Architects borrowed prevalent features of local tobacco barns and corncribs—gable ends, exposed structure, red paint, and cedar board-and-batten siding. Through the screen of deciduous trees, the two-story cottage appears from the front to be just another small, one-story farm structure. Approached from the low side of the hollow and viewed from the side, it resembles a two-story barn, with galvanized metal roof gleaming in the sunlight.

◁ Tucked into a hollow, the cottage looks like a small, one-story building from the road but opens up to long woodland views from the private deck on the side.

△ Taking cues from the site, the cottage has a stone base, a wood middle, and a roof that enfolds the house like an arching, forest canopy.

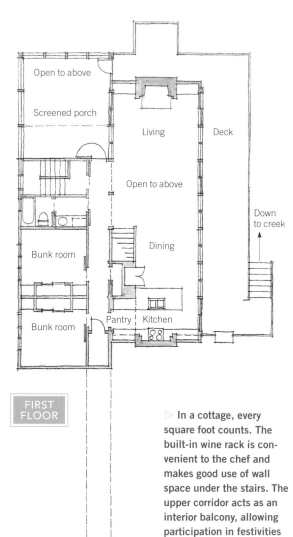

▷ In a cottage, every square foot counts. The built-in wine rack is convenient to the chef and makes good use of wall space under the stairs. The upper corridor acts as an interior balcony, allowing participation in festivities from both floors.

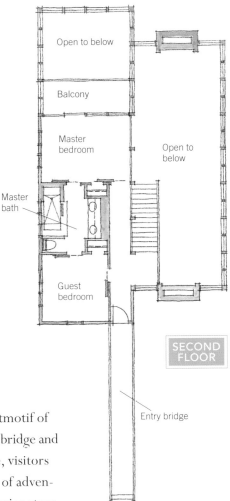

△ The entire cottage is transparent yet private. The interior glass walls of the first-floor screened porch create an away space without sacrificing view. The concrete floor of the porch floor is not only water resistant but also cool and refreshing under bare feet.

Floor plan labels:
- Open to below
- Balcony
- Master bedroom
- Open to below
- Master bath
- Guest bedroom
- SECOND FLOOR
- Entry bridge

In Touch with Nature and History

Transparency and connection to nature are the leitmotif of this cottage. The entry road parallels a natural stone bridge and overlooks a mountain stream. To enter the cottage, visitors cross a suspended footbridge, which lends a sense of adventure to the arrival and eliminates the need for exterior steps.

The front door is on the upper floor, and the view from the entry hall is down a cascading stair to an airy, double-height room richly appointed with a wood ceiling, glass walls, and a soaring, dry-stack graystone chimney. Together with another stone chimney at the other end of the open two-story area, the chimney bookends the living, dining, and kitchen space. The tall interior columns create the illusion that the forest marches right into the house.

James and Diane's family has lived in this part of Tennessee for three generations, and history is important to them. When an old train shed was demolished in Nashville, they salvaged the wood for the 18-in.-wide floor planks and the massive wood mantels.

▷ Cottage living allows everyone to pitch in. This well-appointed Pullman kitchen connects to all the activity, and its proximity to the deck encourages everyone to help carry dishes in and out. The cook can talk with family members coming and going through the front door above.

▷ Distressed wood, bubble glass, and rough-hewn mantel and stone bestow a rustic patina on the up-to-date kitchen. The stone wall and stove hearth bookend the working fireplace on the opposite wall of the great room.

Inside Outside

All of the main living spaces connect directly to the outdoors. The upper corridor is really an interior balcony, overlooking the activity in the family area below and looking out through the tall wall of windows to the woodland beyond. As you move along the balcony, you can almost imagine that you are walking among the treetops.

The window wall faces northeast, and three of the glass panels actually are doors that open from the living, dining, and kitchen areas to a large treated-pine deck. Almost invisible against the forest backdrop, the wood and wire-rope rail of the deck allows an unimpeded view of the woodland from inside or out. And if bugs overstay their welcome, a double-height screen porch connected to both the living room and deck provides a welcome refuge.

The Cottage Fireplace

{ Inside & Out } A cottage brings you that much closer to a
simplified world of earth, wind, and…fire.
The fireplace has always been an important part of the cottage
and often was its primary source of heat. Today, very few cottage fireplaces provide more than supplemental heat; their
function, instead, is to add a warm atmosphere.

Fireplaces can be made of masonry and/or steel, but the
elemental nature of the cottage dictates a fireplace surround
of indigenous stone or hearty brick. In this example, ashlar cut
stone is set into rectangular chimney walls that bookend the
cottage. The stone relates to the rocky setting and is a natural,
local material that geographically defines the kitchen and
living room.

Local stone is the appropriate aesthetic choice for the fireplace, just as the well-engineered steel firebox and the exposed
steel flue were the right functional choices. This cottage, like
many in its locale, is built of local stone foundations and
capped with metal roofing. The pairing of stone fireplace inside
the cottage and steel flue above the metal roof is compatible
with that look.

△ The series of wood columns and beams suggests the simple structure of local corncribs. The contemporary, glassy exposure faces north to minimize glare and heat gain while providing an uninterrupted view of the landscape.

▷ The transparent walls of the master bedroom bring light and views into the gathering spaces without sacrificing privacy. From the upper corridor, the parents can keep an eye on the front door, the living room, and the kitchen without having to run up and down the stairs.

Spacious, Gracious, and Cozy

James and Diane like to host holiday gatherings. The cottage is spacious enough to entertain friends graciously and at the same time cozy enough for a family retreat. The open and integrated living spaces are flexible enough to accommodate a confidential chat by the fireplace, even during a large gathering. In contrast to the large, open great room, Tom Bauer of Bauer Askew proposed giving each generation its own snug private space. Two "bunk" bedrooms and a bath for children are on the first floor. The adults use the second-floor guest room and the master bedroom and bathroom. When James and Diane wake up, they see the forest through the floor-to-ceiling northern glass wall of their bedroom. And to the west is their private balcony, which overlooks the double-height, screened-in porch. The couple loves that the cottage feels as open as the forest, while giving each family member a cozy nesting spot.

The stone tub in the master bath comes as close to a dip in nearby Foster Falls waterfall as you can get. The play of light and shadow across the planes of sculptural stone artfully suggests a rocky setting. The small windows perfectly frame a forest view.

The two-story 16-ft. by 20-ft. screened porch is on the southwest side of the cottage. It combines depth and height to shield the master bedroom from late afternoon glare and heat.

Light and Breezy

This slender, cerulean blue cottage is all about relaxation. Sally and David bought the property because they can easily get to it for weekend getaways. They asked the architects to design a comfortable cottage where they could unwind and soak in the sun.

Like other colorful cottages lining the narrow, pedestrian-friendly streets in the neo-traditional planned community of WaterColor, on the beach in the Florida panhandle, Sally and David's charming two-bedroom cottage borrows from the vernacular Creole cottage style of the 1800s. Set directly on the street and close to its neighbors, the board-and-batten-sided cottage with its standing-seam galvanized metal roof is two rooms wide and two rooms deep with 10-ft.-high ceilings. The public rooms are in the front and the private rooms are to the rear.

Living in the Tropics

The architectural firm Historical Concepts integrated time-tested features of the Creole style to adapt the 1,150-sq.-ft. cottage to its tropical environment. The 300-sq.-ft. front porch is 13 ft. deep and extends the full width of the house

◁ The broad front porch is the first of several hospitable places to sit and socialize at this beach cottage. From the porch, you can see all the way through the cottage to the verdant, inviting backyard.

A BREATH OF FRESH AIR

△ **Color sets the tone for this aptly named planned community; the refreshing blue hues of the porch and swing evoke the water and shadows in a watercolor painting.**

Air-conditioning changed the face of architecture, allowing bland, sealed, glass boxes to be built without reference to their local climate and site. But before air-conditioning was popularized in the 1950s, the various extremes of climate around the country spawned architecture that was distinctly representative of its region. In the American South, with its intense sun, heavy heat, merciless humidity, and profuse insects, settlers responded especially creatively. Here you find projecting eaves, large porches, tall and abundant windows with louvers for maximum cross-ventilation, and metal roofing to reflect the sun's heat.

Today, the renewed emphasis on all things sustainable, earth-friendly, and energy-conserving has revived interest in regional design solutions that are environmentally responsive. This cottage combines new technology and state-of-the-art electrical, plumbing, and other services with a time-honored response to setting. The projecting eaves create a well-shaded porch. And the unusually high ceilings—10 ft. 1 in. throughout—allow for clerestories, louvers, and transoms that maximize natural cross-ventilation while retaining privacy.

▷ **Brightly painted and low slung, this Creole-style cottage is built close to the street and to its neighbors. Native plants subtly screen the front porch from traffic on the street and passersby on the crushed-shell walkway.**

to take advantage of prevailing breezes. The roof has a deep overhang to bathe the porch in shade. Adirondack rocking chairs and a swinging loveseat make the porch a perfect place to let the afternoon slide into evening. Ceiling fans keep the air flowing, and overhead lights make the porch a popular place late into the night.

A trio of double French doors meld interior living space with the front porch. The center set of French doors, the official "front door," brings breezes into the long corridor that flows straight through to the screened sleeping porch and lush yard at the back of the house. Transoms are built into every doorway, exterior and interior, so that cool air and light can circulate freely even when doors are closed for privacy.

Louvered shutters and transoms are time-honored devices for providing privacy, ventilation, and weather protection for homes in tropical locations. Not merely ornamental, the shutters on this front porch fully cover the glass doors and windows and can be securely locked in place.

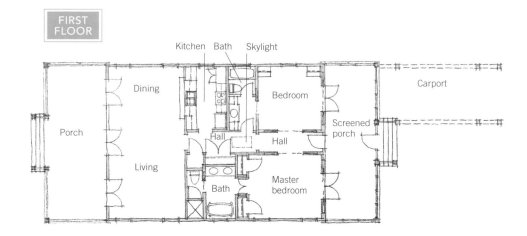

Kitchen Bath Skylight

Dining

Bedroom

Carport

Porch

Screened porch

Hall Hall

Living

Bath Master bedroom

▷ The predominantly white cottage interior comes alive with splashes of rich colors. The cranberry-colored dining room chairs, blue hutch, black wrought-iron chandelier, and glowing floors create a hospitable atmosphere.

◁ Beaded-board walls, patchwork upholstery, and glass-fronted cabinet doors faced with chicken wire lend a casual country feel to the cottage. Painting the cabinet interiors a dark color creates a flattering visual backdrop for colorful glassware.

▽ The sloping threshold creates a smooth transition between the front porch and the living room. Yellow pine floors, sea grass floor coverings, board-and-batten siding, and a painted porch floor add up to beach appeal.

Throughout the house, 10-ft. ceilings and tall, narrow, operable windows help vent hot air and direct airflow. Porch ceiling fans and 2-ft.-deep fixed louvered wood shutters above the porch screens enhance air circulation. And tall, five-panel sliding pocket doors to the bedrooms can be opened fully for cross-ventilation without stealing a bit of floor space.

Casual and Carefree

The combined living and dining area is a contemporary version of the Creole cottage's traditional two front rooms. Casual, white-painted beaded-board walls surround the room, capped by a simple cornice at door and window height. A soft blue band floats above the cornice like a cloudless sky, emphasizing the tall ceilings. Highly varnished yellow pine floors glimmer against the white walls for a clean, informal look.

An eating counter/buffet and overhead cupboards separate the kitchen from the dining area. Recessed under-cabinet lighting illuminates the high, black countertop, which screens the kitchen workspace from view while maintaining a sociable connection to the living-dining area. A beaded-board kitchen pantry continues the vintage look.

All the service areas—kitchen, utility room, laundry closet, master bathroom, and child's bath—are sandwiched in the center of the cottage, reserving the front and back views for living room, dining room, and bedrooms.

IN THE POCKET

{Nooks & Crannies} A pocket door, which slides into and out of a recess built into a wall, is a great solution when you have too little floor space for a swinging door or there is no wall for a door to rest against when opened. Pocket doors like this one are popular because they provide great openness when retracted yet yield great privacy when magically extended from their secret hiding places.

The best thing about the pocket doors in this comfortable cottage is the way they've been used to

further the design intent. By their placement, they reinforce the plan organization while increasing the functional versatility and visual connection of the adjacent spaces.

◁ Sleeping on the back porch is cool and comfortable in these hammock beds, which are suspended by chains from the ceiling and can be anchored in place with floor hooks. With the ceiling fan whirring, curtains can be drawn across the screens for privacy without any loss of airflow.

Sweet Dreams

One way to keep life carefree is to limit how much "stuff" we bring along and surround ourselves with. The master bedroom has two small closets, each only 8 sq. ft. A clothes chest at the foot of the child's bed takes the place of a closet. Both bedrooms are deliberately kept plain, with white beaded-board walls and white cotton Roman shades over tall, rectangular two-over-two sash windows.

Limiting the colors to blue and white and employing simple geometric patterns imparts a restful feeling to the master bedroom. The beach theme of the cottage is enhanced by the woven straw headboard, the matching chair, and the hurricane-style reading lamps. In the child's bedroom, a playful sailboat motif and candy apple red and white color scheme lend a delightful zing.

Hands down, the best place to catch the breeze is the sleeping porch. Attached to both bedrooms by double French doors, this 200-sq.-ft. room captures the serene cottage feeling of drifting off to sleep without a care in the world. Gauzy curtains and wood shutters provide privacy without shutting out the early morning bird songs and the first morning light.

Cottage dreaming is something many of us enjoy. David and Sally find that actually dreaming in your cottage is much sweeter than just dreaming about a cottage.

△ Combining basic geometric patterns—checks and stripes—with elemental white wood trim and detailing bestows a restful and comforting atmosphere in the master bedroom. The large, circular mirror reflects light, making the room seem larger.

◁ Whimsical headboard ornamentation is a fun way to make a cottage bed a place of vacation dreams and memories. The boats sailing across this headboard are joined by a treasured model sailboat silhouetted in the square, porthole-like window.

The deck floats 2 ft. above the ground, using a large rock as a stepping stone. The 160-sq.-ft. deck with built-in seating adds almost 50 percent more living space to the 400-sq.-ft. cottage.

Living Lightly on the Land

For many years, architect A. Richard Williams spent his summers sailing the Great Lakes. When the time came to move ashore, he set out to find an appropriate piece of land for a cottage on Michigan's Upper Peninsula. To his delight, he spotted this old-growth cedar grove on the shores of Lake Michigan, where the constant sound of waves and wind is music to a sailor's ears. He had to convince both the property owner and the zoning appeals board that he could design and build a cottage that would literally disappear into the woods and not require removal of a single tree. Dick fulfilled his pledge. Lightly placed among the trees and floating above the forest floor, the cedar and glass summer cottage with pyramidal metal roof is almost invisible to first-time visitors.

Like the Ojibwa tribes who preceded him, Richard leaves Michigan in the fall and travels throughout the winter. Well into his sixth decade of architectural practice, he has simplified his life so that his architectural studio, salon, sleeping area, kitchen, and bath all fit into his one-room, 400-sq.-ft. cottage. The cottage design reflects his love of the sea and

△ Receding into the shadows of the old-growth cedar grove, the contemporary, dark-toned metal and glass cottage is one with the natural landscape. The wood piers supporting the cottage touch the ground at only eight points, like tree trunks.

△ The building materials of this Michigan cottage and small guest cottage—iron, stone, and wood—were drawn from the abundant natural resources of the area. The steeply sloped roofs easily shed the heavy winter snows.

△ Inspired by a ship's galley, the kitchen takes up no more space than it absolutely has to, and meal preparation is kept simple. The narrow window offers shelf space and gives the cook a view of the lake.

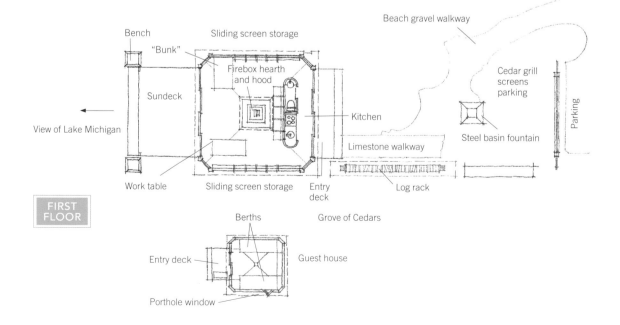

Bench
"Bunk"
Sliding screen storage
Beach gravel walkway
Firebox hearth and hood
Sundeck
Cedar grill screens parking
Parking
View of Lake Michigan
Kitchen
Work table
Sliding screen storage
Entry deck
Limestone walkway
Log rack
Steel basin fountain

FIRST FLOOR

Berths
Grove of Cedars
Entry deck
Guest house
Porthole window

respect for the land; the interior dimensions are as tight as a ship's hold, and the building occupies not one more inch of land than was absolutely necessary. Dick named the cottage "Singassin," which is Ojibwa for "song borne on the wind." A separate 80-sq.-ft. guesthouse snugly sleeps two. As dark and compact as a ship's hold, the tiny, black-painted cottage has portholes for windows.

▽ Just like a bird's nest, the small cottage fits snugly among the trees. The metal roof is notched to accommodate the lean of a tall tree, and the wood deck was built around the trunk of another.

WHAT'S IN A NAME?

The inspiration for cottage names can come from any number of sources. It is said that the typical new subdivision is named for the natural amenity that was destroyed to make way for its development. Cottages more often are named for amenities that continue to characterize the area and that the cottage owners cherish. Some owners choose a name that describes the scenic or historical location or the unique pleasures of the place. Others borrow from local tradition, nature, or both. "Singassin," which means "song borne on the wind," is a perfect name for a cottage in storied Ojibwa territory where the wind can be heard whistling through the cedars.

A cottage name may have a special, more private meaning for the owners. It might allude to an important event or a family tradition that the owners want to perpetuate. Typically, cottage names are personal, maybe even secretive, representing inside jokes and endearing associations—perhaps a child's mispronunciation of the name of a nearby attraction—that the family can enjoy privately for years to come.

Landlocked and Shipshape

The efficient organization and tightly detailed interior of the main cottage is strongly influenced by boats that Dick has designed and built himself. Encapsulated in a 6-ft.-long, cedar-sided curved wall are the highly well-ordered one-person kitchen galley and the bathroom. A 1-ft.-tall horizontal shuttered cutout just at eye level runs along the length of the booth, borrowing light from windows and keeping a glimpse of the lake in sight. Slim Venetian blinds can instantly cover the northern wall of windows for privacy from the drive and parking spaces.

The interior reflects local natural resources, with its finishes of cedar and limestone, birch and iron. The pyramidal ceiling is composed of exposed rafters and cedar decking. The 4-ft. by 4-ft. metal firebox hood suspended from the ceiling's center point hovers like a lowered ceiling, defining the salon area. The all-in-one glass dining, coffee, and cocktail table sits on a heavily fossilized limestone slab from a

△ For many people, cottages are a creative haven, not somewhere to get away from it all. Creativity comes with some clutter; these gridded pine and paper doors attractively screen a full wall of storage.

◁ The interior of the cottage reflects the exterior in materials and shapes. The suspended firebox hood evokes the cottage roof, cedar is used inside and out, and the stone floor is crafted from the stone of the pathway.

Little Brother

{ Inside & Out } Cottages may need to be updated and enlarged to accommodate friends and expanding families. But adding extra bedrooms, baths, or even a study may be done at the expense of the privacy and intimate scale that make the cottage so special. Building a guest cottage nearby can add capacity and still retain the main cottage's intimacy and personality.

Many guest cottages show a family resemblance to their bigger brothers. In colors, theme, and materials, this guest cottage, named "Niji" (little brother in Ojibwa), is a scaled-down version of its nearby larger sibling. At 64 sq. ft., it provides just the essentials for sleeping and solitude. A fair-weather corridor of overhead cedar connects it to the main cottage and shared services.

▷ The soft gray deck color demonstrates the effects of rain, sun, and snow on cedar; it contrasts with the warm tones of the cedar interior floors. When the sliding glass doors are open, the living room extends to the horizon line.

△ The reflecting water feature resembles an upside-down version of the cottage roof. Behind it you can catch a glimpse of the guest cottage, a building so tiny that a porthole is used for the window.

△ The experience of leaving is as important as arriving at a cottage. The curved kitchen wall gracefully choreographs departures, ushering visitors out to a panoramic view of the landscape. A dark retaining wall and a fence of vertical pickets screen the elevated parking spaces.

local quarry. Floor-to-ceiling Shoji screens conceal wall storage. The delicate paper and gridded wood screens form a unifying backdrop for the theater of the single-room cottage.

Cedar floor planks radiate out from the corners of the limestone slab. The subtle change in flooring direction demarcates the different areas studio, sleeping, and salon—without the need for dividing walls. After so many years of waking up on a sailboat, it was only natural for Dick to position his bed to capture a view of the lake when he wakes.

Inside Outside

The cottage design takes full advantage of the cooling breezes and the gorgeous sunsets over the lake. The south and north glass walls slide open completely and the wood floor flows seamlessly out to the deck, giving the North Woods cottage the look and feel of a lanai, or outdoor living room. Late summer meals are enjoyed on the deck, where 2-ft.-wide built-in benches are wide enough to be used both as seating and as a dining ledge. From the water's edge, it looks as though the cedars are protecting this tiny cottage and guesthouse, almost as if they were there first and the trees grew around them.

△ Here's cottage living at its best. One step outside and you are enveloped in sun, wind, and water, with room to stretch out and dream.

Simply Grand

The first time architect Bob Luchetti toured Hugh and Susan's 19th-century beach cottage, he was struck by how dark and dreary it was. He recalls that the entire cottage was painted battleship gray, the ceilings were a uniform 8 ft. high throughout, the windows were small, and the only interior lighting was from small table lamps. The owners asked Bob to open up the rooms to take advantage of the great views of Long Island Sound.

The beaded-board walls and ceilings and the pitch-pine floors were original to the cottage. These typical and humble cottage materials set the tone for the renovation. At 2,950 sq. ft., this three-bedroom, three-bath cottage is a grand old dame in the 19th-century tradition of American summer homes. Blending these themes, the owners and their architect agreed the remodeled cottage should be "simply grand."

◁ Dramatic double-height spaces are generally reserved for grand entry halls. In this cottage twist, the two-story breakfast room, which opens to the garden court and herb garden, is flooded with natural light. Lowered ceilings over the kitchen workspace create a room within a room.

Hitting the Right Note

Every successful renovation project has one big idea that makes it sing. The decision to create a two-story clerestory in the living room by enclosing the northern portion of the second-floor porch and removing large sections of the second floor itself got the rhythm going. The next high note was hit when the interior staircase walls were replaced with a wood picket banister. The soaring three-story staircase energizes the center of the cottage. With light from a chorus of openings, the entire cottage was transformed from a warren of small, dingy rooms into a bright, airy space where all three floors gracefully flow into one another.

The custom wood base, door, window, crown, and cove molding were designed to match the Arts and Crafts character of the 19th-century beaded board. The battleship gray paint is gone, replaced by soft yellow, muted green, and rosy pink walls accented with bright white trim. The original pitch-pine wood floors were stripped and refinished to a high gloss. Bob replaced the formal six-over-six and six-over-one Colonial Revival windows with oversized two-over-two windows and multiple sets of French doors, giving the cottage a more intimate look while bringing as much light as possible into the living spaces.

The clerestory created an opportunity to open up the couple's second-floor master suite. Hugh and Susan enjoy being alone at the shore; when they have the cottage to themselves, there is no need for their bedroom to be

△ Keeping in character with the 19th-century tenor of the cottage, the bathrooms are spare and simple.

◁ This sunny yellow Colonial Revival cottage, along with its neighbors, evokes images of long-ago summers spent lounging and reading on porches, with the fragrance of old-fashioned Rosa Rugosa roses wafting up from the beach.

Stairs that Frame a Special View

{ Inside & Out } Many cottages don't even have them, but for those that do, staircases can be more than just vehicles to get from floor to floor. Stairways don't have to be impenetrable barriers with opaque walls of beaded-wood siding or drywall. They can be opened up on one or two sides to share a special view with the entire floor, spread light through the cottage, and make the rooms seem larger.

In this simple and elegant example, the walls have been peeled away to reveal views of Long Island Sound beyond. An interior oak handrail caps 1x1 white balusters that mirror the exterior porch rails, and the entire stair has become a transparent sculpture that ties together the cottage's three levels.

◁ Tucked securely under the master suite balcony, the living room is an island of repose. The hearth of green glazed tile is the visual knot that the ribbons of indoor-outdoor, up-and-down activity swirl around.

completely enclosed. A sitting alcove off the bedroom now extends over the living room, enclosed by a rail and banister that match the stair. Translucent glass sliding doors can be drawn behind the alcove to make the bedroom private. Because there are no neighbors on the beach side and the second-story porch is 20 ft. deep and roofed, there is no need for drapery or shades. Hugh and Susan can enjoy the entire vista of the Sound from their master suite, and at night they can watch the lighthouse beacon sweeping the shoreline.

▽ The low ceiling in the master bedroom heightens the impression that the windows and French doors are oversized. The doorsill is extra high—to keep out any wind-driven rain—while cooling breezes flow into the balcony and bedroom.

▽ The once-spare maid's bathroom retains its simple charm with beaded-board walls and original sink. The colorful and cushy upholstered built-in window seat and bookshelf add warm and comforting accents.

◁ Cottages enjoy flexible living spaces. When the sliding frosted-glass doors are open, the master bedroom opens up to the living room below. When shut, the bedroom is private.

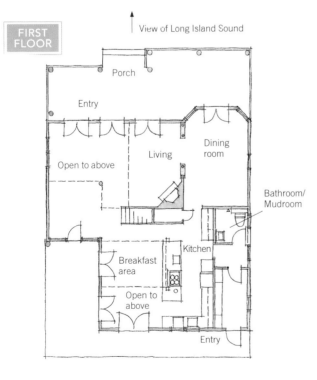

FIRST FLOOR

↑ View of Long Island Sound

Porch

Entry

Open to above

Living

Dining room

Breakfast area

Kitchen

Open to above

Bathroom/ Mudroom

Entry

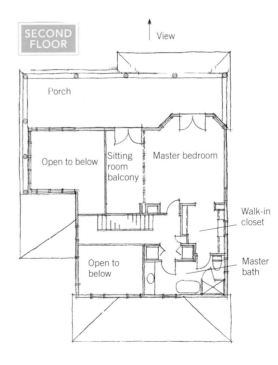

SECOND FLOOR

↑ View

Porch

Open to below

Sitting room balcony

Master bedroom

Open to below

Walk-in closet

Master bath

△ Colonial Revival columns and a transfer beam replace the support originally provided by a bearing wall that was removed to open up the dining room. Simple wood picture frames match the color and tone of the dining set.

△ This outdoor room can be enjoyed morning and evening, seven months of the year. The stone flooring absorbs the heat of the sun's rays, and the cottage walls block winds blowing off the Sound.

BEDDING DOWN

[Nooks & Crannies] Whether large or small, there comes a time when a cottage does not have enough bedrooms. When that happens, some cottage owners break out sofa beds, futons, trundle beds, or Murphy beds that mysteriously come out of the wall. Others colonize outdoor decks and lofts accessed by ladders. Best of all are the moving walls and large sliding doors that combine subtlety with cottage utility to yield more space options.

A lot of cottages start as open bunkhouses with rows of bunkbeds sharing open space with the kitchen. Since many cottages are Spartan and utilitarian, privacy is often a low priority. The reverse can also be true. When the visitors return to the city, a terrace door can be opened or a partition rolled away so that a master bedroom becomes a large, private space once again.

A Brighter Pavilion

To fit with the 19th-century feel of the cottage, the architect custom-designed the kitchen cabinets using individual door and drawer fronts on vertical stile and rail–faced boxes. The couple enjoys entertaining, and their emphasis is on good, simple meals that bring the conversation to center stage. Small-diameter low-voltage lighting is recessed into the ceilings throughout the cottage; each light is outfitted with a dimmer. With the twist of a dial, the ambiance of the room changes from bright to romantic. Generous task lighting is recessed into the low ceiling over the counter and cooktops. When the lighting is dimmed, the working part of the kitchen disappears into the shadows. Romance lingers in the air all day long, from breakfast on the bedroom balcony to whispered late-night conversation on the front porch.

Active Season

An avid golfer, the owner of a resort site hugging the Chechessee River marsh in South Carolina presented his architects with an interesting challenge: Design a vacation cottage where four people, who may or may not know each other well, can feel at home and enjoy a golf outing. James Strickland, Terry Pylant, and Zhi Feng, of the Atlanta architectural firm Historical Concepts, were one shy of a foursome, but they clearly understood the lay of the course.

The architects designed a two-story, 2,900-sq.-ft. golf retreat cottage, combining social and private spaces. From the front door, inviting living rooms are immediately visible. The spacious entry hall and the combined living and dining room encourage the free flow of movement and conversation. Front and back porches totaling a generous 640 sq. ft. round out the casual social spaces. After a long day of golf, dinner at the resort's clubhouse beckons; the cottage's compact galley kitchen fills the bill for breakfast and light meals.

◁ This new Carpenter Gothic cottage retains all the charm of its 1840s ancestors. Steeply pitched cross-gabled roofs, vertical board-and-batten siding in white wood, and the perfectly symmetrical plan are hallmarks of the style.

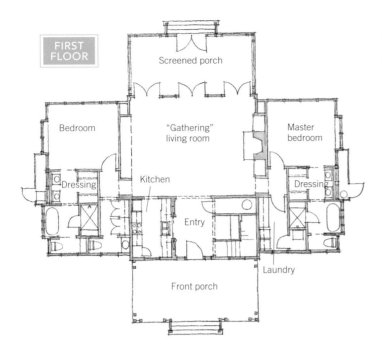

Screened porch

Bedroom

"Gathering" living room

Master bedroom

Dressing

Kitchen

Dressing

Entry

Laundry

Front porch

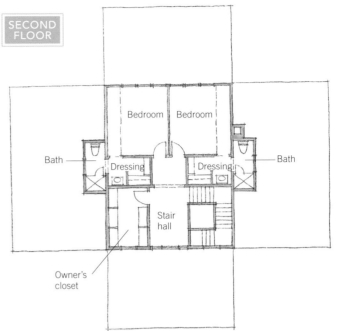

Bedroom

Bedroom

Bath

Dressing

Dressing

Bath

Stair hall

Owner's closet

The owner requested that each of the cottage's four bedrooms—two on the first floor and two on the second—be very private so that each guest would have a quiet place to call home during a golfing getaway. Each bedroom has its own full bath and dressing room. On the first floor, the bedrooms nestle under sloping roofs on the sides of the cottage. A powder room/coat closet, a laundry room, and the stair hall buffer the bedrooms from the entry. The upper bedrooms are smaller but share all the amenities of the larger rooms.

The upper portion of the stair hall is designed as an out-of-the-way place where guests can read or catch up on e-mail. Since this is a vacation cottage, the architects included a secure "owner's closet" under the eaves, where personal items can be stored when the owner is not part of the foursome.

Carpenter Gothic Redux

At almost 3,000 sq. ft., the cottage is large, but the owner wanted it to look small so as not to dominate the landscape. The steeply sloping cross-gable roofs disguise the full second story of the cottage. The true scale of the woodland cottage is camouflaged by the tall, slender poplars surrounding it and by the high, leafy canopy.

△ **Each of the four bedrooms has its own walk-in closet and connecting bathroom. Efficiently laid out and well appointed, the closets leave the bedrooms unencumbered by storage areas, which allows them to be larger.**

△ High, deep-set clerestory windows free up one wall for placement of a voluminous bed. The adjacent window wall provides a pastoral and private view of the creek and marshes beyond.

△ Simplicity is a cottage hallmark. The 8-ft. ceilings, unadorned transom windows, and austere walls provide a soothing backdrop for a long, hot soak in the antique-style porcelain claw-foot tub.

△ This is a golfer's cottage, and golfers need a comfy place to remove their golfing shoes. The built-in bench just inside the front entry is an inviting place (and a polite reminder) to take off the spiked shoes right away to safeguard the heart-pine floors.

The architects had fun bending the rules of the Carpenter Gothic style, composing a contemporary rendition with simplified details. Even though the same design elements—white wood, brackets, rafters, and finials—are used all around the cottage, no two elevations are exactly alike. The gabled front entry, with its strict symmetry, board-and-batten vertical siding, hood molding over the windows, corrugated sloping metal roofs, bargeboards, and pronounced brackets, is the most historically accurate. The rules are relaxed on the less formal elevations, where the layered battens suggest a geometric siding pattern and the window detailing is simplified. On the marsh elevation, brackets are reduced in size but increased in number to create a lively look. Crooked finials atop each gable end have a witty, come-hither quality.

Southern Hospitality

The interior of the cottage, with its flexible seating spaces, large gathering table, and open atmosphere, radiates hospitality. Wood is the major interior material, as is fitting in a Carpenter Gothic cottage. The rich, dark tones of the

KITCHEN INCOGNITO

{Nooks & Crannies} Standing in the entry to this cottage can be a transforming experience. When the louvered pocket doors are closed, the foyer is a wide and dignified passageway to the great room. But open the doors and the foyer connects to the kitchen...or becomes a watering hole with its own wet bar!

What is revealed beyond the opening is a well-designed kitchen with a serving surface that forms a polite buffer between food station and guest area. Black stone counters, elegant base cabinets, overhead cabinets of distressed wood, and complementary colored tile backsplash serve this efficient, convenient, not to mention petite, kitchen.

There is a historical precedent. When Mme. de Pompadour, mistress of King Louis XVI, hired Ange-Jacques Gabriel to design the Petit Trianon at Versailles, disappearing was a major design criterion. A concealed dumbwaiter was employed to hide both the food and the people who prepared it. The disappearing kitchen in this cottage is handled with enough flair to make every guest, even a king, feel pampered.

◁ The steeply angled second-floor dormer topped with a finial gives the contemporary rectangular window the pointed arch look of historic Carpenter Gothic cottage windows. The transom windows along the sides of the cottage bring light to the first-floor bedroom and bath suites.

△ A variety of local woods—heart-pine floors, painted poplar walls, and bleached poplar wood ceilings—bestows an elegant and vernacular timbre to the dining room. The oak and painted furniture reflects South Carolina's rich history of furniture craftsmanship.

For Cottage Swingers

{ Inside & Out } The porch swing makes an ideal perch for capturing summer breezes and savoring summer experiences. Porch swings first became popular more than 150 years ago when time was still slow and genteel. In today's fast-paced world, the porch swing provides an enduring connection to those slower times.

Porch swings have changed, though. Victorian swings were made of wicker. Today, teak, cedar, and other woods sealed in paint are popular materials. Distinctive markings usually are confined to the back supports, which may be curved or at the very least shaped for comfort.

The swing shown here is fairly typical, with an angled bench seat that floats about 18 in. above the porch floor, suspended from the ceiling by chains and hooks. At more than 5 ft. long, this one's the perfect size for one or two people, but swings can be much bigger: We know of one in Nebraska that seats more than 20!

△ At twilight the assorted window details—from the hood molding over the center windows to the square windows punched out of the second story to the transom windows over the front doors—create a lively and bright welcome.

textured heart-pine floors speak of old trees, and the pale, silky poplar wood walls and ceilings tie in with the poplars growing outside the tall porch windows. A soothing celadon green, white, and butternut yellow color scheme weaves all the rooms together. Following southern tradition, many of the moldings are painted a glossy white, bringing inside the crisp look of the exterior.

Cottage living would be incomplete without a porch or two for outdoor living. An overhanging metal roof shelters the wide front porch from rain and the midday heat. Ceiling fans keep the 300-sq.-ft. back porch cool and comfortable in the still of the day. And the back porch is screened so that after a day on the golf course, guests can come out, relax, and enjoy panoramic views of twilight over the Chechessee marsh.

Fabulous Prefab

Not all cottage dreams are about a picturesque little gem with peaked roofs, diamond-paned windows, and an icing of gingerbread detailing. This home-owner's dream was to create a contemporary modular pre-fab cottage that could be put up anywhere, on any site, and at an affordable price, while retaining the quality of design, the intimacy of scale, and the meaningful connection to the landscape that make cottage living a delight.

The owner asked Vetter Denk Architects to design a two-bedroom, three-bath cottage, then built the prototype on a narrow, steeply sloped lot on the shore of a lake near his Milwaukee home. Since the cottage is so close by, he and his family love inviting friends over to take the cottage for "test drives" on weekends.

The 2,200-sq.-ft., three-story cottage is the color of gingerbread, but that's the closest it comes to 19th-century architectural gingerbread. The first glimpse of the modern, rectilinear, machine-engineered, flat-roofed cottage alerts you that this is not your grandmother's cottage. A second glance reveals that the glass window walls were specifically designed to reflect the beauty of the ever-changing

◁ Standardization of construction reinforces a strong architectural composition and keeps costs down. The component pieces of this prefabricated cottage are clearly visible in one glance, as is the view through the building to the scenery beyond, in itself a cottage design hallmark.

surrounding landscape like a state-of-the-art video screen. Just as steamboat technology inspired the design and location of cottages, this structure announces the arrival of factory-manufactured cottages.

Precision Placement

The cottage is a sleek, streamlined package of prefabricated components precisely calculated to deliver 18,000 cu. ft. of interior volume, 670 sq. ft. of outdoor balconies and porches, 52 lin. ft. of closet and shelf space, and 900 sq. ft. of glass openings. But the design proves that precise does not always translate into cold and sterile.

Warm Douglas fir siding nicely offsets the crushed granite walkway and cool, serene bluestone entry paving. A richly toned mahogany door opens to a friendly living space, where the kitchen, living, and dining rooms are encircled by lake

△ **In an open plan, implied boundaries create rooms. The living room is defined by the alternation of MDF and glass panels. Pendant lights and sliding glass doors to the covered porch define the dining room.**

COTTAGE PEDIGREE

COTTAGE PREFAB

Many 19th-century cottages were located in wilderness areas, where building materials were scarce or inferior. Because the cottages were used as second or occasional homes, their construction tended to the basic and utilitarian. Many were crude structures built from prefabricated panels that could be shipped by boat to sites otherwise inaccessible and erected quickly by semi-skilled locals. Mail-order gingerbread detail often was added.

In the 20th century, the size and diversity of our geography, the great variety of building materials, and the nature of labor and building laws sidetracked the United States from developing prefabricated components as major building materials. Now, in the 21st century, prefabrication

has attracted new support as a way to control rising construction costs. Demand for prefabricated housing continues to grow, fed by concern for improved quality, speed of construction, and a renewed interest in the modern machine aesthetic.

The prefab parts for this cottage were delivered to the site on a flatbed truck, and within 48 hours the shell was in place. Built on a 4-ft. by 4-ft. grid, the cottage is composed of a series of 8-ft. by 20-ft. exterior wall panels. Each panel has an integral structural core faced with prefinished cedar plywood, with vertical battens to cover the joints. The wood floor components lock together to span the floor beams and provide the formwork for the colored, poured-in-place concrete with embedded radiant-heat piping.

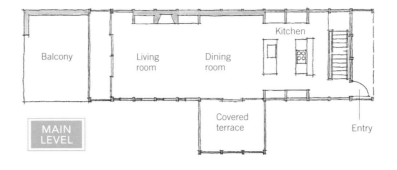

▽ The large glass end wall draws the lake view into the living room. The polished concrete floor mimics the color and sheen of the lake's surface; it contains radiant-heating coils that warm the cottage without the intrusion of vents.

Balcony

Living room

Dining room

Kitchen

MAIN LEVEL

Covered terrace

Entry

and woodland views. The open and flexible design accommodates both intimate gatherings and large parties that can spill out onto the two terraces. The three glass walls of the main living level give the small cottage an expansive feel. The one solid wall runs the full length of the cottage, forming a backdrop for built-in kitchen appliances, open shelving, and a large-screen television built in over a gas fireplace.

An almost transparent stair leads the way to the top floor, where two bedrooms have ultimate privacy. Each has its own bath and access to a private balcony. Clerestory windows float above ocher-toned medium-density fiberboard (MDF) walls, affording a view of ancient oak treetop canopies. The bedroom walls dissolve into horizontal wood shutters on the master bedroom and hallway balconies.

The lowest level houses the laundry and utility room, a full bathroom, and an entertainment room that doubles as a

▷ **The blond butcher-block kitchen countertop does double duty as a dining buffet. Kitchen appliances and shelving are recessed slightly to reduce their visual impact from the living and dining areas.**

LOWER
LEVEL

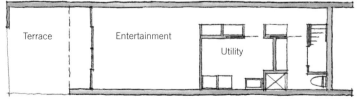

Terrace   Entertainment

Utility

◀——— To Moose Lake

▷ **Nature is more exotic from the low vantage point of the platform bed. The lake's horizon line is at eye level, and the night stars appear higher in the sky when seen through the clerestory windows that float just under the ceiling.**

A Cottage for a Car

{ Inside & Out } There is a reason why garages spawn high-tech startups and rock bands. The typical garage reduces its architecture to a Spartan shell that offers little diversion from the act of creating.

This cottage garage has a modern simplicity that suggests both class and quality. It matches the main cottage in its prefab design and materials, making it more a guest cottage for the car than just a garage. The long tandem layout with garage doors at opposing ends maximizes utility by providing separate zones for a multitude of chores. The standard garage doors are outfitted with multicell polycarbonate panels to bring a glow of daylight into the garage and send a fluorescent glow out at night.

▷ Built to look like the corncribs on nearby farms, the slatted wood porch takes the 17th-century concept of framing the landscape in a picturesque manner into the 21st century.

△ Invisible from the front of the house because of the sloping site, the lower level opens directly to the lake. Dripping swimsuits do no damage on their way to the laundry room since the interior floors are low-maintenance colored concrete.

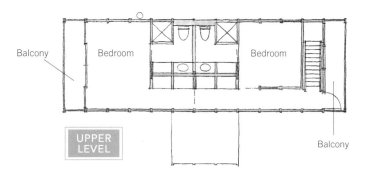

Balcony

Bedroom

Bedroom

UPPER LEVEL

Balcony

guest room. Sliding doors open to a concrete terrace overlooking the lake. The concrete-block retaining wall works as a privacy screen, sheltering the covered terrace.

Finding the Right Exposure

The architects nicknamed the cottage "Aperture House" because of the cameralike way each window grouping frames outdoor views of the lake and the ancient trees. Rising from the steeply sloped bank, the expansive glass walls present a kaleidoscopic view of nature.

The owner wanted the glossy, high-style design to be energy efficient. To keep costs down for maintaining the

△ This modular porch looks as if it could slide in and out of the cottage like a drawer. The exterior board-and-batten siding and the open slats direct cooling breezes into the living room.

glass-walled cottage, the design needed to minimize heat gain and loss. Sliding out like a puzzle piece from the living room, a porch with louvered walls and ceiling acts as a sunscreen, cutting down on heat gain. Throughout the cottage, insulated ceilings keep heat loss low, and low-maintenance honey-colored concrete floors contain radiant heating coils that keep the rooms toasty at little expense.

Second homes are more popular than ever, and the lament that "all the good sites are gone" resonates in vacation areas. The beauty of this cottage prototype is that it is designed to adapt to difficult site conditions, fitting onto properties someone else might pass by. The narrow, 4-ft. on center rectangular module with concrete-block lower level is easily adaptable to variations in slope. Just point the narrow ends to the best views, keep the solid wall to the north and a window wall to the south, and "click"—you have a great shot at cottage living.

◁ Evocative of an old 4 x 5 camera bellows, the exposed columns, deep beams, and clerestory windows in the hallway create a dynamic rhythm of light and shadow.

◁ Is it a cottage or a cabin? The log interior of this cottage might give credence to the claim it is a cabin, but the high design and luxurious touches definitely make it a cottage.

Victorian Gothic

I n 1850 A. J. Downing, landscape gardener and author, wrote *Victorian Cottage Residences,* one of the most successful books on cottage design and still in print today. Downing promoted the cottage as a style that would improve domestic architecture and give the owner a new source of enjoyment of rural life. He would heartily have applauded Mark and Shirlene's efforts. Every Friday, as soon as they can get away from their demanding jobs, the two leave Atlanta and head north to their Victorian Gothic-style cottage in the Smoky Mountains.

Both Mark and Shirlene wanted a cottage that was rustic in appearance and offered indoor-outdoor living but also included the comforts of a resort. Mark is an avid fly fisherman, so a site with a watercourse was a basic requirement. The site they found has not only a trout stream but wooded slopes and a dramatic, sheer granite mountain wall as well. Combined with the cottage itself, it is an idyllic answer to their dreams.

▷ The vertical roughsawn weathered cedar siding lends an air of antiquity to this newly constructed mountain cottage. Porches on two levels provide multiple opportunities to enjoy the outdoors.

△ Rough-finished walls, unpainted wood window trim, and the distressed wood shelf disguise a modern whirlpool tub and create the feeling of being in another place and another time, if only for a long weekend.

The simple, vertical wood exterior of the gabled cottage is very much in character with Downing's premise that the rustic style is the best fit for rural settings. On the interior, the two-bedroom, 2,300-sq.-ft. cottage combines hand-hewn beams and collectible furnishings with such deluxe features as heated towel racks and whirlpool baths. For indoor-outdoor living, it has 1,280 sq. ft. of porch and deck space. There are stone fireplaces both inside and on the deck.

The beauty of natural materials is expressed throughout the cottage and the grounds. The varied hues and textures of the luxuriant entry landscaping set the tone. Sheltered beneath the Gothic porch roof, double doors of weathered wood with four panels and hefty brass handles welcome guests. In the entry foyer, a "rug" of hand-painted floor tiles reflects the Downing-approved combination of beauty and utility. Wide, old pine planks make a silky smooth floor surface throughout the cottage, and the stone hearth in the great room radiates warmth long after the fire is reduced to glowing embers.

△ The yellow pine floors and the red-stained tobacco barn siding enhance the cottage's affinity with the rural mountain region. The square of inset, hand-painted floor tiles warms the entry hall like a rug.

△ The dramatic interplay of textures and materials adds interest to large volumes. Ceiling spotlights wash the various wood finishes and stone with light. The curved iron rebar balcony rails add a rustic feature to the romantic second-story overlook.

Everything Old Is New Again

The couple enlisted many local craftsmen to contribute to the construction of their cottage so that it would be one of a kind. As an example, the stonemason rebuilt the fireplaces twice to get just the right look of rusticity.

Mark collected most of the wood used inside the cottage from an old tobacco barn in northern Georgia; other wood came from a Kentucky horse barn. A sawmill owner came out of retirement to cut the lumber exactly to Shirlene's specifications. The interiors of the logs were used for the stair treads, the stringers, and the kitchen counter, and the old beams were trimmed to 2 in. to 3 in. thick and used as paneling. The large scale of the panels and chinking adds grandeur to the two-story great room.

During Shirlene's years of working as a photo stylist, she collected furniture and other decorative objects, and her collection lends a regional flavor to the cottage. The entire kitchen was designed around the glass-fronted, yellow-painted wood pantry. As a special anniversary present to themselves, the couple splurged and bought an antique soapstone sink for the master bath.

WINDOW SEATS

{Nooks & Crannies} The window seat can probably trace its lineage to the 17th-century Turkish "sofa," a raised and boisterously cushioned seating platform inset in a wall or surrounded on three sides by windows. Often the Turkish sofa was located at the terminus of an important room or even on an ample stair landing where natural lighting and views were desired and needed.

Today's window seats satisfy our desire to have the security of structure and enclosure and still be able to see what's going on around us. In this respect, window seats are a microcosm of all that we appreciate in a home or cottage.

The bucolic window seat in this cottage has it all: the comfort of built-in upholstered seating, with maximal storage below and full views into the room and to the outdoor world.

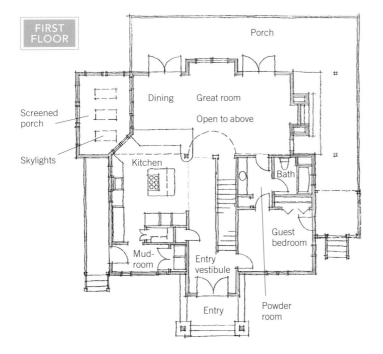

FIRST FLOOR

Porch

Dining

Great room

Open to above

Screened porch

Skylights

Kitchen

Bath

Mud-room

Guest bedroom

Entry vestibule

Entry

Powder room

◁ **This bathroom is designed to appeal to touch. Smooth beaded-and plank-board walls contrast with the rough wood cabinet and forged metal handles. The hand-crafted soapstone sink wears the patina of age gracefully.**

▽ **The coppery glow of the dishwasher front and the faucet fittings lends the look of an antique photograph to the fully up-to-date kitchen. The couple's collection of vintage cooking utensils adds to the old-fashioned flavor.**

▷ Just large enough for a daybed, sink, and potting table, the potting shed is a unique structure crafted of timber framing infilled with round wood "tiles" and concrete. The small scale of the shed provides a nice contrast to the sheer granite wall beyond.

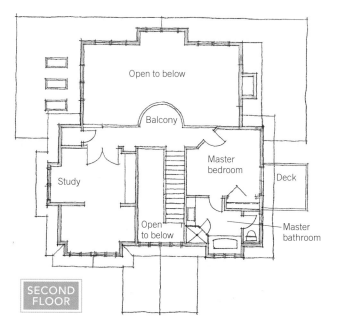

SECOND FLOOR

Open to below

Balcony

Study

Master bedroom

Deck

Open to below

Master bathroom

In Close Contact with Nature

Large, operable windows are stacked on the south-facing side of the great room to bring the outdoors in. The large wraparound porch is directly connected to the great room via twin French doors. When Mark and Shirlene have large gatherings, guests wander freely from the great room to the open porch and the screened porch. The kitchen, ornamented with Shirlene's collection of vintage cooking utensils, is part of the open plan. The counter often doubles as a buffet.

The couple's favorite spot is the seating area in front of the outdoor fireplace. It's cozy even in the winter and especially at night. With this porch, Mark and Shirlene can enjoy the outdoors no matter what the weather; a 10-ft. overhang keeps it dry. On sunny days, light flows through three skylights in the porch roof, chasing away the early morning chill and keeping the area bright and welcoming all day long.

▷ Even though the building is brand new, recycled barn wood, antique furniture, and old methods of construction help create the feeling that this cottage is old and seasoned. New French doors open the dining room to the porch, but their deep mahogany stain blends with the seasoned look.

◁ Cottage traditions such as outdoor dining, sitting, and rocking are still much enjoyed, especially when they take place in front of an outdoor fireplace where a trout stream can be heard rushing by.

COTTAGE  PEDIGREE

THE DOWNING COTTAGE INDUSTRY

Landscape designer Andrew Jackson Downing (1015 1852) could be considered America's first arbiter of taste. He was a leading advocate of straightforward cottage dwellings for workingmen and their families. Downing's *Victorian Cottage Residences* used handsome illustrated examples by architect Alexander Jackson Davis to show how American cottages could rival the cottage homes of England as models of affordable, sensible design.

Downing was hardly original, but he was the most successful cottage proponent to communicate to a wide audience that no person of taste could consider designing a cottage without taking into account the "lay of the land and the design of the grounds." An ardent proponent of the "picturesque," Downing applied the same principles to evaluate the aesthetic effect of landscape gardens and architecture: harmony, balance, elegant simplicity, truth, and the beauty of utility.

The cottages A. J. Downing wrote about were not always small vacation getaways. Many were large homes by today's standards, and they were intended to be in towns, villages, or even, as he says, suburbs. His prototypes range from simple wooden houses for families of moderate means to elaborate Italianate stone cottages for more prosperous households, but they all serve as excellent examples for today's cottage.

The Upside-Down Cottage

◁ A delightful collection of gable ends clusters together to form this beach cottage. The "garage" contains a golf cart and bicycles, which, along with walking, are the preferred modes of transportation on this island getaway.

t took the owners of this cottage just one visit to the island off the Carolina coast to decide they wanted to live there, at least part time. On their second visit, they purchased a lot and hired architects Chuck and Anna Dietsche to design the cottage and its interiors. The owners lead busy professional lives and needed to be able to hand over the aesthetic reins of the project to a firm that could do everything for them, top to bottom.

Seen from a distance, the cottage looks as though it's all roof and gable end. The wood shingles, the white wood trim, and the grouping and banding of windows epitomize the hallmarks of cottage architecture. Close up, the small details say that this cottage was specially designed for people who love it. Anna and Chuck design many summer homes and enjoy the opportunity to continue the coastal tradition of cottage architecture.

To take advantage of the ocean views, the architects turned the cottage upside down, putting the living area on the second floor. With this topsy-turvy arrangement, the three first-floor guest rooms are shielded from the southern

SECOND FLOOR

Bath
Master bedroom
Kitchen
Living room
Balcony/Porch

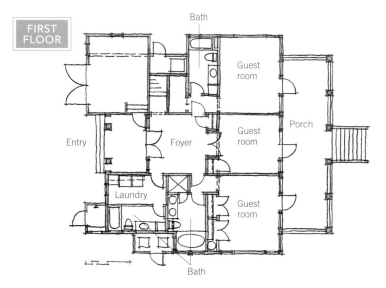

FIRST FLOOR

Bath
Guest room
Guest room
Porch
Entry
Foyer
Guest room
Laundry
Guest room
Bath

△ The cottage has three porches, one for every occasion and view. The first floor houses the guest bedrooms, each of which opens to this sheltered porch. Guests can spend some quiet time here without worrying about disturbing the owners.

sun by the overhanging porch roof. Guests have direct access to the covered porch from their rooms. The spacious entry foyer offers a warm welcome, with a faux-painted sky and painted floor executed by a local artist. The first-floor plan pays homage to the cottage tradition of small, spare bedrooms and to the time-honored nine-square grid favored by classical architects.

It Pays to Practice Your Scales

To get built on the island, a cottage has to be at least 1,300 sq. ft. and care has to be taken not to block any other residents' views of the water. The couple wanted their cottage to be large enough for a crowd but also comfortable for just the two of them. The placement of guest rooms on the first floor and master bedroom and living spaces on the second floor accomplished that goal.

△ The exposed windows in the master bedroom capture light and views; white roll-down shades provide privacy. The porch rail floats away from the column, architecturally going with the flow of relaxed coastal living.

◁ The painting in the foyer, one of the couple's favorites, sets a relaxing tone. The first-floor laundry room is accessible to everyone in this cottage, where easy maintenance carries the day.

△ The master bedroom is located directly off the living room; seen through double French doors, it looks like a sitting room. Interior windows bring light into the living room and can be opened to allow sea breezes to flow through the cottage.

▷ An intimate kitchen was important to the owners. To achieve this, the architects used vertical beaded board with a natural finish under the steep slope of the dormer, creating a kitchen that is denlike in feel.

This extra-deep sink cuts down on splashing water, eliminating the need for a backsplash. The counter is wider than standard, so there is plenty of room for both a sink and table setting. Folks on both sides of the counter enjoy the view.

The wife is a great cook and enjoys doing the lion's share of the cooking herself. The kitchen is compact—just a tad more than 100 sq. ft.—putting everything within easy reach, and the ceiling follows the slope of the gable, reinforcing the solo-chef scale. The prep island doubles as a dining counter.

On the inside, Anna repeated the banding emphasis used on the exterior. Bright white paint on the trim and molding of both furniture and walls draws the eye up, down, and around the interior, creating a visually active and animated room.

Unwinding

The owners come to the island to entertain, cook, and enjoy a change of pace. With the exception of emergency vehicles, no cars are allowed on the island. Even contractor vehicles have to leave the island by a designated hour. Life is lived at a pedestrian pace.

The couple wants to enjoy a clutter-free life in their cottage. The architects designed classically inspired built-ins, many of which were built by local craftsmen, to define

ONE WALL, MANY NOOKS

{Nooks & Crannies} Every cottage can profit from a sprinkling of nooks and crannies. These small pleasures lend charm to the space, bring scale down to an intimate level, and reinforce the basic appeal of the cottage as the place to change perspective, to reflect, and to appreciate your surroundings.

Architect Chuck Dietsche erected a partial wall in this cottage that articulates many appealing little spaces. Built at an arresting angle to the plan, the striped wall provides visual and functional separation from the floor below. It's also a warm home for the fireplace and creates nooks and crannies galore. Best seen here is a built-in shelving unit for useful and pretty cottage collections. But there's more to the display; with its abundant crown molding, the partial wall serves as both wall cap and additional storage shelf.

To the left of the storage/display unit, above the stairs and not visible from this angle, is a small seating area. Beyond the fireplace on the right is another hidden nook with a small bench for quiet reflection or a tête-à-tête.

△ One way to pick an exterior palette is to study the landscape. The cottage roof reflects the green of the shrubs; the siding echoes the gray of the boardwalk; and the white trim borrows from the clouds, the waves, and the sand.

rooms within the second-floor open plan and keep clutter at bay. The fireplace and the custom-designed entertainment armoire and china cabinet are placed to frame ocean views from sociable furniture groupings around the room. The entertainment armoire is on wheels, ready to go wherever it's needed. Part china hutch, part food pantry, the glass-fronted cabinet provides much-needed storage space while acting as a room divider. The second-story porch adds 180 sq. ft. of social space; the party can spill out of the living room and enjoy views to the water over a stretch of beach and sea grasses.

△ This cottage living room makes a playful statement, contrasting neutral colors with bold white banding to create a highly ornamented interior that integrates the various geometries of the walls and ceilings.

Outdoor Showers

{ Inside & Out } The outdoor shower has come a long way since the days when an old garden hose was hung on the cottage wall or an overflowing rain gutter provided wet relief.

Today's cottage outdoor shower has grown into an evocative luxury with requisite bells and whistles, just as it has grown in demand. No longer just a cold-water spout, it can come outfitted with pressure balancing, with body spas or sprays, with handheld or multiple shower heads on slide bars, or with "towers" featuring multiple heads for different parts of the anatomy or the family. You can even celebrate an occasion with a "champagne spray."

Whether a shower module is trucked in or built on site, for modesty's sake it most likely will be hidden in an adjacent changing room, screened by a fence or an extended wall. Locations for outdoor showers are chosen carefully to provide scenic views while affording privacy from neighbors. Grooved decks and access paths between shower and cottage are put to work as large welcome mats that remove errant sand and grit from wet bare feet, protecting prized interior floors.

{ HIDE-A-WAY HILLS, OHIO }

A Family Affair

Lisa and Greg Cini had already renovated 10 cottages with an eye toward resale, but when they saw this little cottage, they knew right away it was a keeper. On the shore of a lake in Hide-A-Way Hills, a wooded resort community about an hour from Columbus, Ohio, the cottage was a dream come true for a family of four that loves water activities.

Once the 36-year-old, 900-sq.-ft. cottage was theirs, Lisa and Greg took a close look at its condition. Built as a rough-and-tumble weekend fishing cottage, it had only the most basic amenities. They discovered that almost everything from the bottom up had to be replaced, including all heating, plumbing, and electrical services. Along with these updates, the Cinis wanted to improve the cottage to reflect the high standards of their interior design firm, Mosaic Design Studio.

Lisa and Greg had a six-month window in their schedule to design the remodel and complete the construction. The resort community required that they maintain the existing footprint, remove no trees, and give the cottage an exterior color that would blend in with the natural surroundings. Major changes were permitted only inside the cottage.

◁ Cottages come in all shapes, sizes, and colors. This small lake cottage is tall and boxy. Once the cedar siding ages to a silvery gray, the cottage will blend with the lake and melt into the landscape.

101

△ The owners like the way the laminated wood roof structure visually passes through the clerestory, making the living room and porch look like one big indoor-outdoor room. The circular pendant light makes the dining table the center of attention.

Setting the Tone

Typical of many cottages in scenic locations, the living room and a porch of this two-story cottage are on the top floor to capture the best view. The kitchen, dining area, bedrooms, and another porch are below. Lisa and Greg wanted to bring features of the woodland landscape into the cottage as well. They used water, wood, and stone elements to create a harmonious connection to the natural surroundings. The slate on the walls and fireplace reminded them of the colors of the creek bed and river rocks right outside their cottage. To belie the boxy outline of the cottage exterior, the Cinis in-

LOWER LEVEL

View to lake

Porch

Entry

Dining

Kitchen

Bath

serted subtle, organic curves inside—overhead in the light fixtures and soffits, and underfoot in the linoleum floor.

Practicality and a contemporary attitude also were priorities. To set a modern tone, Lisa ordered an ergonomic kitchen from an Italian manufacturer. Mostly steel and wood, the kitchen is beautiful to look at, easy to clean, and streamlined for efficient meal preparation when cooking for a large group. The height of the stove and counters can be adjusted, and the curved surfaces accommodate the comings and goings of multiple chefs. The refrigerator is set into a wall cavity, gaining a valuable 2 ft. to 3 ft. of floor space.

Life on the Water

Because so many of the necessary changes were major, and expensive, Lisa and Greg tried to be prudent when it came to moving walls around. To maximize views with the least reorganization of spaces, Lisa's brother, Jim, who joined the team as master carpenter, proposed opening up the stairwell and rebuilding the second-floor screen porch as a sheltered balcony. With a balcony extension instead of a covered screened porch, the living room feels closer to the outdoors and the lake view is crystal clear.

△ Before the renovation, the stair was completely boxed in and there were no windows on the land side of the cottage. Opening up the stair and adding windows changed the whole feel of the cottage from cramped to capacious.

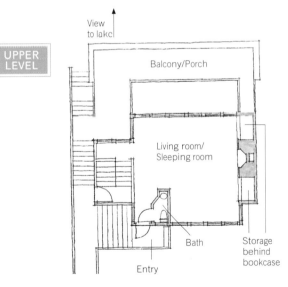

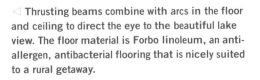

◁ Thrusting beams combine with arcs in the floor and ceiling to direct the eye to the beautiful lake view. The floor material is Forbo linoleum, an anti-allergen, antibacterial flooring that is nicely suited to a rural getaway.

Even in cottages, people worry that the television will dominate the living space and the furniture arrangement. In Lisa and Greg's cottage, a combination of old and new technology solved the problem. For their stone fireplace the couple commissioned a carved wood fire screen and mantel to express their love of water and fishing. These works of art captivate the eye far more than the flat-screen television that is built into the fireplace wall.

At first, the family slept in the bedrooms. The rooms were private, but they were on the land side and were hot

△ The interior of the cottage is only 900 sq. ft., but balconies off the kitchen and living room, two lakeside decks, and a dock provide a wealth of outdoor entertainment options. At the end of the boating and fishing season, boats and gear are stored behind the lattice screen beneath the cottage.

△ The graceful-looking cupboard door is constructed like a lightweight airplane wing, with fabric stretched over a light metal frame. The entire door can be removed, submerged in water and washed.

and stuffy. The family got into the habit of dragging mattresses up to the living room to enjoy the breeze. Everyone would drop off to sleep listening to stories and to the sounds of the lake.

When her son commented that this was his favorite part of staying at the cottage, Lisa purchased futons that look like conventional couches and at night unfold into full beds. Someday, when the kids are older, the Cinis may add a third floor for bedrooms, but for now they all enjoy camping indoors together.

Getting There Is Half the Fun

{ Inside & Out } Because of the growing demand for cottage property, people are traveling greater distances to find their ideal cottage getaways. The farther and more challenging that quest, the more appreciated it is. In a time when getting there is half the fun, getting to this hideaway has the appearance of being a major expedition.

Siting close to the water removes the cottage to the far reaches of the property. To reach the cottage, you have to cross a sequence of elevated wood decks, paths, and stairs that descend toward the water, floating over the landscape like a path through the Everglades. The panoply of surrounding trees and plantings heightens the atmosphere and sense of anticipation, which is relieved only by reaching the lake and the cottage floating above it at journey's end.

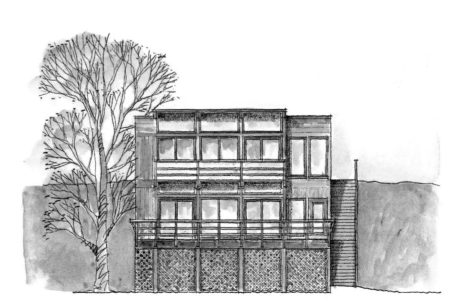

◁ **Built-ins are space-saving devices that come in especially handy in a small cottage. These built-in bookshelves were designed to swing out, revealing additional, but invisible, storage. The sloped roof and ceiling add drama on the interior and help shed water on the exterior.**

Kids Only

◁ The elevated porch of the guest cottage tops a covered walkway that is a great place for staging luggage and sports equipment while packing or un-packing the cars. A welcoming view of the main cottage is framed by the porch, stairs, and cottage wall.

When families get together for holiday meals, kids often enjoy dining at their own table, where cloth napkins can give way to paper and less-than-perfect table manners can be overlooked. The owners of this summer cottage went a step further when considering multigenerational logistics at their Long Island Sound beachfront property; they decided to add a stand-alone rustic cottage—a place where their grandkids can be kids, dirty socks and play equipment are part of the orna-mentation, and if beds go unmade, grandmother will neither know nor care.

The couple hired architect Bob Page to design the guest cottage. Bob has designed a number of cottages in the area and knows about the ins and outs of cottage life, as well as about such practical issues as setbacks, flood plains, septic systems, and designing for a waterfront environment. Over the many years the owners have been coming to their Shin-gle Style cottage, they have seen many old summer cottages torn down and replaced by large, year-round homes. The owners wanted to keep the look and tradition of "summer

only," back-to-basics living alive in the design of the kids' cottage and also wanted the new cottage to fit comfortably with the main cottage.

View from the Tower

The guest cottage is not just a miniature of the main cottage, although Bob used several similar elements—cedar shingles for walls and roof, the broken cornice, white-painted trim, and six-over-one double-hung windows—to link the two buildings. The guest cottage is simpler than the main cottage, almost minimal in its form and ornamentation, so that, although the cottages clearly belong together, the kids' cottage puts a contemporary spin on the Shingle Style.

The garage occupies the ground level of the kids' cottage, and the wood-plank garage doors swing out, much as early garage doors did. The second and third floors of the cottage contain two bedrooms with views to the Sound. Altogether, the three-story tower is a seaside landmark.

△ **The tiny cottage has an intimate dining table and two chairs for sharing a cup of tea or a game of cards. In a small cottage, space is at a premium; here, the antique table doubles as a bookshelf.**

COTTAGE PEDIGREE

TOWER COTTAGES

Tower cottages are raised a level or two above grade to enjoy dynamic views, solar orientation, natural ventilation, greater security, or all of the above. The ground level, which in earlier eras may have housed a stable for horses and carriages, today accommodates cars, boats, or even planes.

Probably the earliest tower residences were medieval structures above livestock enclosures for purposes of security and hygiene. A staple of the English cottage tradition, tower cottages have been fashioned from keeps in Cistercian abbeys and from gatehouses with raised aspects. In one of his books, 19th-century

designer A. J. Downing even describes "A Small Cottage for a Toll Gate House (with Prominent Tower)."

Like Sri Lanka's famous 20th-century architect Geoffrey Bawa, the architect of this Connecticut tower cottage brings together disparate styles in his contemporary designs. Cutting corners on this traditional East Coast cottage envelope is a gutsy structural maneuver. Bawa designed many similarly striking tower cottages that rose above Sri Lanka's often-steep topography and dense greenery to enjoy breezes and distant ocean views.

△ Tower cottages, with living areas on the upper floors, take advantage of distant views. The gray-shingled portions of this tower are living spaces, and the white wood demarcates storage and garage space.

△ The original gabled cottage, with naturally weathered shingles, white trim, and decorative shutters, has been in the family for years. Matching gable ends, trim color, shingles, and six-over-one casement windows enable the new cottage to fit right in.

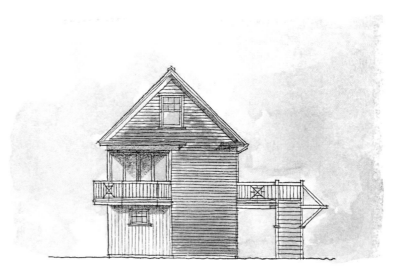

△ A kitchenette occupies a corner of the second-floor bedroom. The thin, horizontal paneling in the sleeping area helps create the illusion that the bedroom and kitchen alcove are separate rooms.

Kids of All Ages

Because the main cottage is where the family spends most of the time, the guest cottage is tailored for quiet times and sleeping. With a tad less than 1,000 sq. ft. of living space, it is intimate in scale. The second floor is where the owners' adult children stay. All the necessities—powder room (baths are taken in the main cottage), washer, dryer, small refrigerator, kitchen sink, and a bedroom with double bed—are on this floor. The grandchildren sleep in a third-floor bunk room.

Like the exterior, the interior finishes reflect the back-to-basics theme. The walls and ceilings are covered with simple pine beaded board and sheathing, all of which are coated with a clear urethane finish that reveals the wood's knots and

Well Vented

{ Inside&Out } A continuous copper vent was designed to run along the ridge of this waterfront cottage. For summertime venting and cooling, this age-old, low-tech option makes a lot of sense.

Because it is intended only for habitation in warm months, the guest cottage has no heating system and consequently needs no insulation. Steel gusset plates laterally brace each of the rafters and take the place of a conventional ridge beam. The resulting void between the rafters and the roof sheathing serves as a simple and direct raceway for the hot summer air. At the roof peak, the heat is expelled through the copper wire mesh and the 2x6 blocking in the rafters.

▷ The amber tones of the pine interior glow when light spills through the two skylights and the cutout above the bunk-room door. Each of the four head-to-toe bunks has under-bed storage and an adjacent closet.

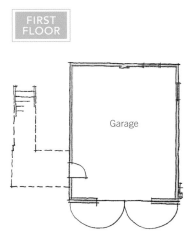

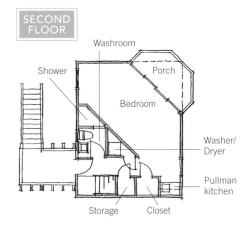

FIRST FLOOR

Garage

SECOND FLOOR

Washroom

Shower

Porch

Bedroom

Washer/ Dryer

Pullman kitchen

Storage

Closet

THIRD FLOOR

Bunks

Bunk room

Skylights

Bunks

Open

Closet

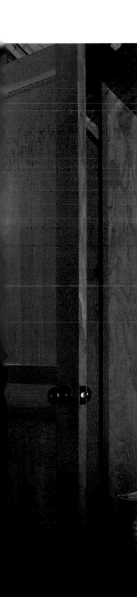

quirks. The ceiling rafters are exposed, and the furnishings are, in cottage tradition, an assemblage of much-loved and much-used family pieces. By our definition, if a cottage isn't romantic, then it's just a vacation home. Bob rotated the second-floor bedroom walls 45 degrees to embrace the romantic vista of the Sound. Sliding French doors open up the entire diagonal wall to a nighttime view of the stars and the moon. A wedge carved from the rectangular cottage creates a void for a covered porch; the cantilevered gable end of the third floor acts as the porch roof, and the bedroom floor extends out for the decking.

Bunk Room

Up one more flight is the bunk room for the grandkids. Four cots, each with under-bed storage, nestle under the eaves. The room has four closets, each large enough for about four changes of clothes. Two operable skylights illuminate the interior closets and increase ventilation. Because the cottage is used only in the summer, insulation is not necessary. The walls go all the way up to the ridge, which is a continuous copper vent, and all of the structure is exposed. The floor is carpeted; remember, the parents sleep one floor below. Lighting is kept to a minimum because when the kids go upstairs, it's time for "lights out." Tomorrow will be another fun summer day.

△ **The second-floor porch of this tower cottage enjoys panoramic views of the Sound. Traditional designs and color were enlisted for the porch rails, to harmonize with the older cottage and other neighboring cottages.**

◁ The bedrooms of this cottage
are small and spare, evoking an
earlier, simpler time. The woodwork and walls are painted
white, showcasing the dark
furniture and providing a comforting contrast to the more
vibrant main room.

{ AUGUSTA, MISSOURI }

History Lessons

The owners of this home are Missouri history buffs, so it is only fitting that they chose an 1850s one-room schoolhouse to convert to a cottage. In 1850 there were just enough farms in the area for recent German immigrants to build a one-room schoolhouse for their children. The school was named Lonesome Glen, reflecting the isolated location. When the land changed hands in 1919, the 1,320-sq.-ft school was moved to its present site and renamed Happy Glen, showing the new optimism of the growing community.

The last class graduated in 1960, and a fire destroyed the old school in 1994. When the couple bought the property to build a two-bedroom cottage, they decided to give some of the history back to the community by re-creating the schoolhouse exterior. Well known for their award-winning large projects, architects Mackey Mitchell Associates of St. Louis enjoyed the change of pace of working on a small, historical building.

▽ Set on a knoll, this former one-room schoolhouse is a landmark in the neighborhood. The honest geometric forms of the cottage hold the promise of traveling back in time to appreciate and savor a simple life.

Ding Dong School Bell

The rebuilt schoolhouse is now a local landmark. The tall bell tower, visible from the clubhouse and fairways of the nearby golf club, evokes memories for longtime residents and offers a glimpse into the area's rich local history for newcomers.

While the design revolves around the spirit of the historic schoolhouse, Mackey Mitchell made a few changes to accommodate contemporary living. Rather than paint the cottage white as it originally was, the owners opted for stained wood that will weather gracefully. A school bell hangs in the yard rather than in the bell tower. That tall cupola now acts as a light and ventilation shaft for the cottage. The weathervane atop the tower is an added touch of whimsy. In terms of comfort, cottage living doesn't take a summer vacation, so air-conditioning has been installed to offer welcome relief after 18 holes of golf.

△ This 21st-century re-creation of a 19th-century school exemplifies three Rs, but they are the Rs of recycling and restraint that go hand in hand with renovation. The column and bench, salvaged from another 1850s building, are authentic down to the cracks and dull finish.

School Bell to Light Well

{ Inside & Out } This cottage project started out as a renovation of a single-room schoolhouse. A subsequent fire did not prevent architect John Guenther of Mackey Mitchell Associates from designing a cottage derived from the concept of a schoolhouse and updated for today's cottage living. The basic palette remained: wood siding, exterior stone fireplace, lean-to for kitchen services in the rear, and porch.

But how to justify the belfry sitting prominently on the pyramidal roof in this modern adaptation? Where the ringing bell had once announced the school day to children, the belfry as a light monitor uses the sun's light to announce the time to the cottage occupants today. The pyramidal tower finished in beaded board captures the sunlight and spreads its light below.

△ The main room of the cottage is 900 sq. ft., spacious enough for a kitchen, dining area, living area, and even a baby grand piano.

▷ The cottage celebrates features of the region: The fireplace is constructed of Missouri limestone and the painting over the mantel is one of many works by contemporary local artists that are displayed along with local antiques.

Bedroom

Living room

Cupola above

Bedroom

Porch

Kitchen

Developing Character

When guests arrive, they are surprised to see how much of the schoolhouse character remains yet how well the building works as a cottage. The main room continues the one-room tradition, combining kitchen, dining, and living areas in one 30-ft. by 30-ft. space with a bell tower as its central focal point. The two bedrooms and baths are located in a lean-to addition that draws its form from area structures built by German settlers. Careful attention was paid to how interior design decisions would affect the look of the exterior. Curtains were not used because, seen through the windows, they would have compromised the integrity of the schoolhouse image.

The generous dimensions, soaring ceiling, and long views through tall, double-hung windows in the main room create a spacious, airy environment. The mixing and matching of warm colors and textures, local art, historical photographs, and school-style desks and chairs make this renovation amazingly comfortable; it definitely doesn't have the stiff feeling of a museum setting.

◁ Because the schoolhouse was destroyed by fire, the cottage was a re-creation rather than a preservation project. Fortunately, the old school was well documented, so the architects replicated the siding style, roofing, and windows of the original structure.

The simple interior finishes summon up the warm but no-nonsense style of early schoolrooms. Beaded-board wainscoting and whitewash walls encircle the room. The same beaded board faces the interior of the bell tower. At the top of the tower, four windows bring in light throughout the day. All the windows and doors are simply trimmed in plain, flush pine molding. The Prairie-style cherry kitchen cabinets provide enough contrast to set the dining space apart from the open living room.

Tucked into a recessed corner, the white refrigerator and stove blend into the wall. The sink is placed in the top of a large counter that looks as though it might have been the

△ The sturdy, wood library table is placed where it can drink in light from a pair of large four-over-two windows. Oversized windows like these in the original schoolhouse channeled daylight into the center of the 30-ft. by 30-ft. room.

COTTAGE PEDIGREE

MY OTHER COTTAGE IS A TREE HOUSE

Good design seasoned with a wry sense of humor allows the owners of this "raccoon clubhouse" to expand traditional cottage functions to include what they've dubbed "land sailing." The clubhouse provides ample viewing opportunities of the surrounding forest—and of the neighboring raccoons that gave the structure its name.

Architect John Guenther (of Mackey Mitchell Associates) and his family built their whimsical tree house using a blend of traditional wood siding, shakes, and wood trim...plus a touch of space-age plastic. The ground level,

which meets the change of grade with a suspended drawbridge, provides screened space and seating for several kids, with ladder access to the floor above. This upper deck is splayed to provide backrests for seating, and the clear corrugated plastic arch, or sail shelters the treetop-viewing getaway.

The architectural tradition of the *folly*, in which architectural icons like this combination of portal and garden pavilion are used to extol nature in a personal way, is handled here with élan.

teacher's desk. Two globe pendant lights provide good task lighting and pleasing illumination when the counter is used as a dining table.

The re-created schoolhouse cottage draws from the land for its character. The sheer size of the stone fireplace suggests that it is the main heat source of the cottage, as it would have been for the schoolhouse. It does make the cottage cozy and warm but supplements a modern heating system. The stone is local, and the mantel was carved from a large red oak that fell in the yard during a storm, following in the tradition set by the early German immigrants not to waste anything that could be made into something beautiful.

△ A clear varnish lets the beauty of the pine beaded-board walls shine through. The glossy varnish, the white walls, and lamplight highlight the vintage photos.

◁ Basic white kitchen appliances blend with the walls to create a neutral backdrop for the warm, cherry kitchen cabinetry. Items stored in the island are accessible from both kitchen and living room.

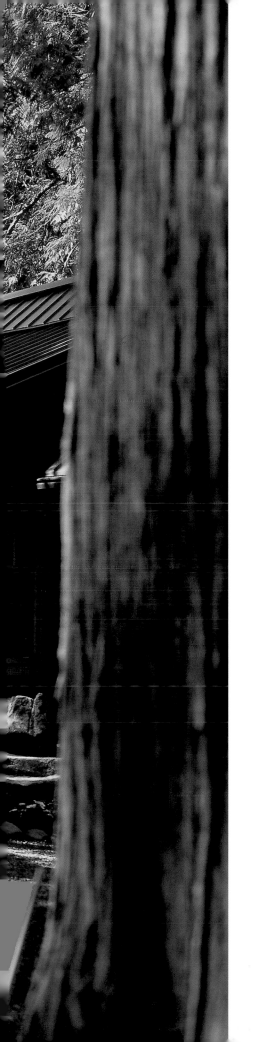

Family Connections

Barbara and Kit spend their winters in the Southwest, but when the temperature starts to rise, they head north to their little red cottage on the banks of glistening Pipe Lake in cool Washington State. It's a change of scene and a change of lifestyle; all winter they enjoy golf, and at their lakeside summer cottage they revel in water activities and gardening.

Barbara's parents bought the cottage property at the height of the Depression for $10 a square foot. Her architect father designed the 996-sq.-ft., one-bedroom summer cottage and scraped together $750 to build it. Many years later, when Barbara inherited the worn and tired property, she knew the cottage needed updating. All the architects she consulted advised her to tear it down and rebuild. Giese Architects' reconstruction proposal best fit Barbara's directive that the new cottage reflect the Scandinavian design influence of her father's original design. At 1,365 sq. ft., the new one-bedroom, one-bath cottage with open-plan kitchen, living, and dining room is a little larger than the old one, but the board-and-batten exterior, painted a cheery red and white, evokes typical Scandinavian cottage design.

◁ The original footprint of the cottage dates from the 1930s. Each addition, expressed by a different roof height and pitch, marks a chapter in the owners' lives. The cottage design borrows from the Scandinavian heritage of the owner.

◁ The picturesque lake view is framed by the double-hung bay windows. At night, four strategically placed recessed ceiling lights highlight the dining area. The two-over-one windows give seated diners a transparent view of the lake.

▽ A wall of built-in bookshelves and Craftsman-style cupboards, a soaring stone fireplace, tall pine pilasters, a rich wood ceiling, and hefty trusses with iron fittings give the great room the warm, substantial feel of a woodland lodge. At night the atmosphere is enhanced by spotlights nested neatly between doubled-up beams.

△ Capping the green-painted cupboards with a knotty pine plate rail implies a lowered ceiling over the kitchen area of the great room, giving the workspace a pleasant sense of enclosure in an open plan. The pine divider with white-painted cap rises out of the countertop to screen the sink and stove from general view.

IN THE TRADITION OF CARL LARSSON

This cottage recalls the uncommon beauty and tranquility of life in a small Swedish village best captured by artist Carl Larsson 100 years ago. Larsson turned his cottage home in Sundborn, Dalarna, Sweden, into a setting for his many illustration assignments. Props for mocked-up drawings became permanent built-ins; his family members served as models; and idyllic summer pursuits were immortalized in his handsome and popular watercolors.

The backdrop for all this was Larsson's picturesque Swedish cottage. Much like the Pipe Lake cottage, it employed traditional hues along with forms and ornament that were simplified and accentuated to achieve what we now regard as a modern aesthetic. Craft details and vivid coloring lent quality to the composition but were stripped down to their essentials for a cheerful, contemporary feel.

The Larsson cottage grew to accommodate his family. The drawing room, indoor and outdoor dining areas, kitchen, bedrooms, studios, and various outbuildings were added, reconfigured, and decorated as needed. Similarly, architecturally distinct elements in the Pipe Lake cottage work together; functional zones such as bedrooms and the dining/living area are separated by entries and punctuated by bay window extensions to turn the cottage into an interactive, village-like composition.

Lake View

Barbara asked the architects to consider views of Pipe Lake when siting the cottage. Large windows flanking the fireplace allow a clear view of the lake through the cottage from the entry patio and front walkway. The overhang of the master bedroom covers the curving paved pathway so that the owners stay dry and mudfree as they come in from the garage.

The cottage is still quite small. Because the great room is only 325 sq. ft., the architects exposed the roof decking above the trusses to call attention to the large volume of the room rather than the small footprint. The hand-built trusses give the room the rusticated look often found in older construction. Three strong elements—the granite boulder fireplace, heavy cedar truss timbers, and views to the lake—reinforce the woodsy ambiance.

△ Upon approach, the quality materials of the slate and stone patio, massive stone chimney, and colorful Dutch door signal an authentic cottage built to last.

FIRST FLOOR

Dining · Kitchen · Gallery · Mudroom · Entry · Bedroom · Bedroom · Patio · Bath · Laundry · Bath · Living

△ Wood window louvers provide both view and privacy, as does the custom-designed fritted-glass shower stall. The beaded-board tub surround and granite tilework add a hint of vintage 1930s styling to the sleek new bathroom.

▷ Storage needs are well met in this cottage with a "gallery" full of easy-access base cabinets, overhead cabinets, and even full-height pantry units.

Transitioning from Part Time to Full Time

Four years after rebuilding the cottage, the couple decided to sell their town home and make the cottage their only Seattle home. They again hired Giese Architects, this time to add a 550-sq.-ft. master bedroom with en suite bath and storage corridor. The master bathroom was custom designed right down to the dimensions of the shower pan. Double sinks and separate bath and shower fit the couple's preferences. A band of slate and glass tiles provides a rich accent to the sun-filled, crisp white bathroom. The original bedroom is now a guest room.

As a weekend getaway, storage was not a concern in the cottage. But the transition to full-time summer living meant that the cottage needed significantly more storage. The architects provided a storage wall along the entire length of the gallery corridor. The Douglas fir cabinets keep linens and cleaning supplies within easy reach and accommodate off-season clothes above. The hallway countertop is a handy place for craft projects and household appliances.

Gray Gardens

Washington is graced with a temperate climate. A balance of hot and cold days and long stretches of gray days marked by rain and humidity ensure that vegetation is luxurious and varied. Barbara and Kit admire the look of traditional English cottages, and they now have the garden of their dreams: an English-style garden overflowing with hydrangea, roses, native grasses and wildflowers, and more than 20 varieties

△ Boaters are treated to a glimpse of the white-trimmed, cranberry-colored cottage from Pipe Lake. The cottage owners enjoy watching waterfront activities from their deck, under the shaded cover of the projecting metal roof.

of rhododendrons, all of which flourish in the Washington climate.

A path of crushed stone leads from the shady front garden to a stone terrace furnished with seating and an outdoor grill. The lakeside garden provides both shade and sun; the shaded slope from the porch leads to a sunny lawn area. Several trees were removed to give the cottage some breathing space, but a large willow that graces the lawn screens the cottage dwellers from view while enabling them to enjoy the scene of boats passing by.

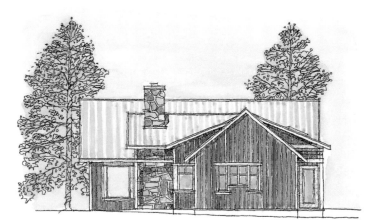

A Warm Welcome

Maine architect Rob Whitten is a firm believer in hospitality, but he was a little surprised that his clients wanted to build their guest cottage before the main house was even under construction. It was early May when the couple asked if he could design a cottage and have it ready for the start of the next school year. The family planned to live in the cottage while the main house was under design review and construction.

Some architects might have balked at the tight timeline, but Rob was intrigued by the challenge and the opportunity. The 12-acre site is beautiful in its diversity. It is on a protected salt estuary, with spectacular water views, seasonal streams, wetlands, and steep embankments. Rob studied the site to find the best locations for the two houses, keeping in mind shoreline and wetland setbacks, solar orientation, and view opportunities. After the main house was built, the cottage would be used as accommodations for visiting family and friends, as a project space, and as a getaway. The family has the satisfaction of knowing firsthand that their guests will be as comfortable as possible.

◁ Careful site analysis ensured that the cottage was placed to take advantage of diverse views and landscape features, and to live lightly on the land, requiring removal of as few mature trees as possible. Light, lacy foundation plantings create a soft transition from landscape to cottage.

Site Lines Tell the Story

{ Inside & Out } Access, solar orientation, available breezes, dominant topography, and distinctive greenery are all important elements to consider in picking just the right spot and name for a cottage.

Often the most important siting criterion is the view of the feature the owners fell in love with. To take best advantage of the view of the Harraseeket River, this guest cottage as well as the main house and outbuildings have been oriented along one unifying south-southwest line. The two-story glazed space in the cottage is designed to capture views of the river and the main house, although the cottage enjoys tranquil seclusion from the main house until the leaves fall in October.

The whole site celebration process is often memorialized in a cottage name. Such sobriquets as Sea View, Cedar Ridge, Sea Breeze, Riverbend, Sound View, and this one, Harraseeket Guest House, tell visitors about a cottage's particular visual character or prized locale.

△ It takes a second glance before you realize that the column supporting the roof is not actually a tree in the forest. Low perennial plantings add color and texture to the view from the porch.

▷ Flowering hydrangea covers a soft green trellis in the summer. The square trellis grid echoes the small, square windows while creating a facade that changes its look with the seasons.

Cottage Orne

The couple told Rob they weren't interested in conventional subdivision houses. They wanted the cottage to be part of the landscape, filled with light and air. Rob took cues from the site for interior and exterior materials. One historical cottage style, the Cottage Orne, seemed appropriate to the site and the couple's limited budget. Cottages designed during the picturesque Orne movement of the late 18th and 19th centuries were often artificially rustic, using timber features in a purely ornamental manner. Rob chose hemlock beams, bark-covered columns, plank floors, board-and-batten doors, and natural pine trim not only to add character to the cottage but also because they were economical. The picturesque theme is part of the landscape as well; a rustic wooden footbridge across a ravine leads to a path to the main house.

△ The warm and hospitable red and green color combination of the cottage's exterior is reflected in the dining table and the weathered hutch. A dollop of each color is just enough to relate the interior to the exterior.

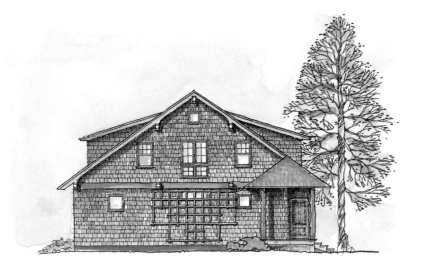

△ Oversized screens and peeled-bark corner columns enhance the indoor-outdoor experience of the porch. The screen openings were designed with a large upper and a smaller lower, and the rail frame is the same height as a chair rail, giving the porch a roomlike feel.

The three-bedroom cottage is 1,450 sq. ft., but it feels and looks more spacious, largely due to the south-facing window wall of the double-height living room. The tall windows frame long views of the pine, hemlock, and oak forest. Two porches, one open and one screened, extend the living space into the landscape, where the family can enjoy the peace and quiet of their woodland surroundings.

Soaring and Sheltering

Entering the cottage is like stepping into a clearing in the woods. Everywhere you look, there are views out to the landscape. The open plan gives the first floor a relaxed atmosphere. Because there are no interior walls, everyone can see what is happening in all areas of the first floor, and conversation flows easily from the sitting area to the kitchen.

▷ The 1,450-sq.-ft. cottage makes a bold statement with a two-story glass window wall that borrows distant views and brings them into the cottage, dissolving boundaries between inside and out and expanding everyone's horizons.

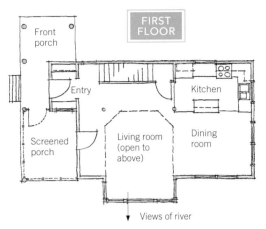

FIRST FLOOR

Front porch

Entry

Kitchen

Screened porch

Living room (open to above)

Dining room

↓ Views of river

BALUSTER DESIGN

{Nooks & Crannies} "Figure ground alternation" is a fancy term for the play of light and dark, the interchange of void and solid. A good example would be the optical illusion of the wine goblet shape that, when reversed, reveals a woman's profile. This graceful and well-detailed stair takes the idea of figure ground alternation to its simplest and most elegant fruition, with 1x6 balusters that are saw-cut to create the illusion of elaborate spindles in their void. A 2x4 fir handrail in natural wood sits comfortably atop the balusters.

◁ First impressions are important. From the front door, the richly variegated pine newel post and stairs are the first things a visitor sees. The warm tones and whimsically detailed balusters say welcome, relax, and enjoy.

Different ceiling heights add variety and interest to the open plan. At the front door and the entrance to the screened-in porch, the ceilings are a standard 8 ft. high. The sloped ceiling of the great room soars to the peak of the ridge beam. The ceilings return to 8 ft. in the kitchen and dining area. The generous landing at the top of the stair works as a balcony that projects over the living room, allowing guests to preview the activities in the room below.

As open as the cottage feels on the interior, the exterior gives the feeling of shelter. Approached from a footpath of crushed stone, the first view of the cottage is of its many rooflines—the low, beckoning roof of the entry porch, the angle of the gable end, and the slope of the great room's projecting bay. The wood shingles are painted a rusty red that contrasts nicely with the green of a leafy summer and stands out warmly in a winter snow, just like a cottage in a child's fairy tale.

△ Kitchen cabinets painted a warm loden green are accented with naturally finished wood grabs. The darker tone defines the kitchen recess and gives it a distinct personality in the open-plan cottage.

△ The views from the cottage are constantly changing. Depending on the season, the estuary is more or less visible from the screened porch. This southeastern corner is a glorious place for breakfast and late summer dinners.

◁ One strategy to buy more space in a small cottage is to have all the living spaces open to one another. The illusion of separate kitchen, dining, and living rooms is created by the spacing of the hemlock columns and the varied ceiling heights and window sizes.

Cooling Sea Breezes

◁ A rosemary hedge and other native plants inside the fenced courtyard emit a sweet, welcoming fragrance at the cottage entry. Elevated, slatted wood boardwalks permit rainwater to be reabsorbed into the ground in a form of passive irrigation.

Rosemary Beach is one of a growing number of neo-traditional towns putting down roots in the once-forgotten region of northwestern Florida. Long known only as a desolate, piney woods landscape, the area is now highly prized for its snowy white beaches, clear blue Gulf of Mexico waters, and mesmerizing sunsets.

Neo-traditional communities employ well-considered guidelines to knit neighborliness and ecology together. Cars tend to be left parked in alleys, because it is so pleasant to stroll down crushed-shell sidewalks lined with drought-tolerant indigenous plants or cycle on the narrow streets and lanes. Wood-plank boardwalks, slightly elevated to protect the fragile beach environment, connect the cottages to each other and to the beach.

It was this ambiance that prompted an Atlanta couple to ask Connecticut architect Robert Orr to design a retreat they could enjoy now and easily convert later to rental units. He came up with an imaginative and animated three-story cottage with a variety of spaces that can be combined to

135

NATIVE INTELLIGENCE

This expertly detailed Florida cottage fits nicely into its traditional neighborhood development by blending the best of local influences and building methods. This palette includes standing-seam metal roofing, wood siding, French doors, high ceilings, and deep porches.

The "cracker house" tradition of the Dutch West Indies and Florida, named for the cracks between floorboards that made it easier to sweep sand off the floors, is alive and well here. The floors, stoops, and porches of this beach house all have widely spaced boards. From the cracker style also comes the use of metal standing-seam roofing to reflect the sun's heat and the distinctive combination of elevated floor, expansive shade porch, and high window and door openings to take full advantage of prevailing breezes and views.

The Sarasota School of Architecture, developed in the 1950s in nearby Sarasota, Florida, blended this same vernacular with the spark of modernism. Houses designed in this style employed products of World War II technology—such as plastic bubble skylights and roofing made of the "mothballing" membrane developed to seal battleships—to create a refreshingly modern look that accommodated the more open 1950s cottage lifestyle.

This Rosemary Beach example blends the best of both approaches. Twenty-first-century technology (plumbing, electrical, and HVAC) has been integrated successfully with the 19th-century vernacular that is site and climate appropriate.

accommodate different guest/rental scenarios. The 2,210-sq.-ft. cottage with garage suite sleeps up to 12 comfortably.

Robert's design inspiration came from the colonial cottages built in the Dutch West Indies in the late 1800s; his interpretation sails smoothly into the 21st century. Like the original Dutch West Indies cottages, this vertical, metal-roofed wooden cottage rises up over the surrounding shrubbery to take advantage of cooling sea breezes and magnificent views. Deep, spacious porches make refreshing seating areas and shield the interior rooms from the strong sunlight.

◁ **Wide porches, muted colors, and interior shutters are signature elements of this beachfront cottage. The main living rooms are on the second floor, there's a bunk room on the ground level, and the master suite occupies the crow's nest.**

◁ The olive-colored cabinets foster a cool feeling in the south-facing kitchen. Louvered double French doors and clerestory windows provide an expansive connection between the kitchen and the covered porch, easing traffic flow when a crowd gathers for dinner.

△ In this cottage community, cars are relegated to alleyways. Fast-growing native plants screen the cars from view at the first-floor level, and cantilevered porches on the second floor channel sight lines directly over the cars to the water.

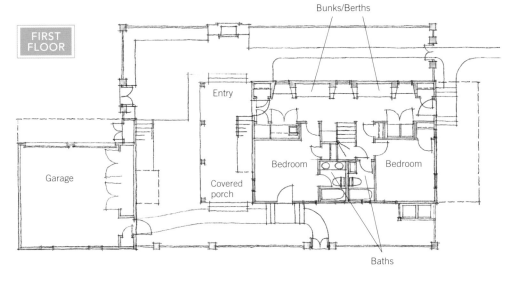

FIRST FLOOR

Bunks/Berths

Entry

Garage

Covered porch

Bedroom

Bedroom

Baths

A SAFE BERTH
IN ANY STORM

{Nooks & Crannies} While this ship of state has found a permanent berth in Rosemary Beach, its plan remains nautical in that it makes the most of every square inch. The spacious gangway that anchors the entry level and first-floor bedrooms does double duty by providing access to midship bunk beds, which are tucked away like "cuddies," or little ship's cabins. The handsome cabinetwork extends the nautical theme, incorporating a ship's ladder in the bulkhead, replete with built-in grab rails above and drawers below for inanimate stowaways.

◁ This cottage enlivens its three-story climb with a staircase that is as grand as a pipe organ. The fun yet sophisticated stair takes center stage— all the other rooms dance around it.

▽ Interior windows surround the staircase, bringing daylight from the third-floor master bedroom and bath into the stairwell; shutters on these windows can be closed for privacy. The green doors turn the clothes cupboard into a design accent.

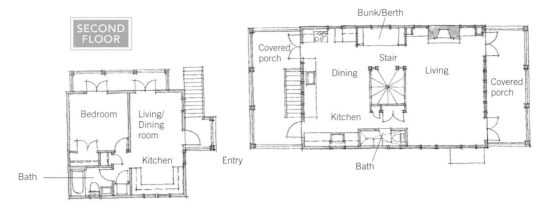

SECOND FLOOR

Bedroom

Living/ Dining room

Kitchen

Bath

Entry

Bunk/Berth

Covered porch

Dining

Stair

Living

Covered porch

Kitchen

Bath

◁ Watching the sunset is a favorite Gulf activity. The open configuration of the top porch rail frames a panoramic snapshot of the skyline, while the closely spaced lower pickets form a privacy skirt for porch sitters.

Sculpted Space

Fine craftsmanship and an artistic eye bring this cottage to life. The sculptural centerpiece is a spiraling staircase. Positioned as the focal point of the cottage interior, the dramatic stair is designed to dazzle from every angle; even the underside is beautifully detailed. A sinuous, black wrought-iron handrail threads through the staircase, accentuating and contrasting with the ordered geometric form and linear, white picket baluster. The stair rises in a U pattern from the ground-floor guest suites to the second-floor living space. From there it spirals up to the third-floor master bedroom and bath suite. Perched under the steeply pitched roof, this personal retreat is surrounded by windows and offers panoramic views of the Gulf.

The expansive windows and broad decks of the living area also take full advantage of the view. The covered kitchen porch is ideal for sunset dining, and the northern living room porch is a shady place to relax during the heat of the day. The

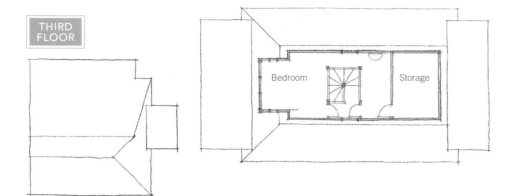

Bedroom   Storage

two porches bookend the living and dining rooms, which revolve around the sculptural stair.

The three-story configuration gives the couple and their guests all the privacy they need. Three separate entrances lead to ground-floor guest accommodations. A double room with separate bath has its own entry off the courtyard. A second suite sleeps up to six—four in a bunk hall and two in an adjoining bedroom. The couple occupies the top two floors, which can be reached by an exterior staircase as well as by the interior stair. A living room window seat can be called into service as a sleeping berth when the cottage is overflowing with guests.

The Test of Time

White wood trim and walls painted butternut yellow reflect the light that spills in from all sides of the cottage. Jewel-toned rugs and dark wood furniture provide a rich contrast to the crisp, light finishes. To reduce heat gain, louvered shutters cover the lower half of the windows, and deep porch overhangs shield the upper panes. A touch of formality is woven into the open living, dining, and kitchen plan, with wood built-ins inspired by the Scottish Arts and Crafts style and an elegant, upwardly curved fireplace mantel.

Rosemary Beach guidelines call for materials and finishes that will look better and better as the cottages age. Rot-resistant wood that stands up to heat and humidity is mandated, and wood stains in earthy tones are encouraged—the stains because they do not fade or peel like paint, and the tones because they are harmonious with wood. The dark exterior of this Florida cottage may come as a surprise to those who associate bright pastel colors with tropical climes. But all the glint and sparkle you could wish for are right outside the front door, where the radiant sun dazzles the white beaches and bright blue water.

△ This cottage was designed with its Gulf Coast location squarely in mind: The lap wood siding is stained, not painted, to withstand high heat and humidity, and the slatted wood stoop lets sand from beachcombers' feet fall through the cracks. The extra-deep second-story porch overhang shades and cools the first floor.

◁ Louvered shutters on the interior make it possible to keep the windows open for breeze while maintaining privacy. The window seat easily converts to a guest bed.

▽ Find the television. It's there but cleverly tucked out of sight behind the lunette doors over the fireplace. The symmetrically placed windowsills flanking the fireplace are deep enough to enclose cabinets and double as seats.

A Cherished American Tradition

Sometimes the best way to make a bold statement is to whisper because everyone will quiet down to hear what you have to say. That is precisely the strategy architect Ross Chapin took in designing this understated 1,300-sq.-ft. cottage in Washington State. The island cottage is a primer in wood cottage vernacular, from the cedar shakes on the gable end right down to the Shaker-influenced knobs on the kitchen cabinets.

Building a cottage out of wood is a cherished American tradition. The warmth and texture of wood are symbolic of a connection to nature, instantly conjuring up a simple lifestyle. The Pacific Northwest is the perfect environment in which to explore the colors, textures, strength, and flexibility of a wide variety of hardwoods and softwoods.

The Art of Connection

Ross's whispering campaign begins with a covered walkway that focuses the visitor's view to the forest while subtly leading to the front door. In a wooded, fairy-tale setting, there is no need to have a massive paneled door to announce entry.

◁ Looking for all the world like a woodsman's hut, the simple wood porte cochère links the outbuildings to the cottage while screening them from view. The front door of the cottage is discovered at the end of the angled and covered pathway.

△ Like the slender, tapered trunk of a Douglas fir tree, this mosaic rubblestone chimney reaches to the sky. Combined with the horizontal siding, the thin taper accentuates the steep peak of the gable.

▷ In the rainy Northwest, covering and crowning the paved walkway keep both visitors and entries dry. At night, when the robust king-pin trusses are lit from above, the approach gleams in golden light.

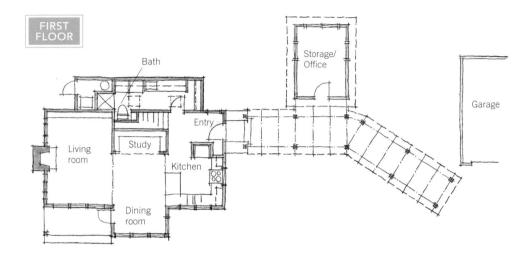

Bath

Storage/Office

Garage

Entry

Living room

Study

Kitchen

Dining room

And by clearly exposing the arbor's timber framing, the cottage's connection to the trees is affirmed.

Washington has a progressive energy policy, and the allowable square footage of glazing is limited by building code. Windows in this cottage are carefully placed to capture the best views, maximize daylight and cross-ventilation, and minimize heat gain. Living in a cottage that works in concert with the microclimate heightens the family's awareness that they live in a specific place, not Anywhere USA.

Smaller Than It Looks

Owners of large homes often trade quality materials and detailing for vastly increased square footage. These cottage owners did just the opposite. The main living spaces of the cottage—the kitchen and living-dining area—occupy a petite 17-ft. by 32-ft. footprint. Both rooms combined are smaller than just one room in many new subdivision homes. In spite of the dimensions, this is hardly an ascetic hermit's cottage. The cherry dining table seats six graciously.

△ Pine frames around windows, doorways, and openings between rooms express a Shaker simplicity matched by the dining chairs. The beckoning, half-open Dutch door is a classic hallmark of Northwest cottages.

▷ **Even in small cottages, variety can be refreshing. Cheery, clear-finished pine frames the opening to the buttermilk-yellow sitting room and calls it out as a restful alcove away from the main flow of cottage activity.**

Going Dutch

{ Inside & Out } In the early 17th century, Dutch colonists to New York's Hudson Valley introduced Dutch doors to America's farmsteads and barns. Originally these were batten doors split horizontally into two halves that could be opened separately. The upper section could be swung out to allow air and light into the interior, while the lower portion was kept closed to keep children safely within and livestock safely out. As the Dutch door was adopted across the United States, a shallow shelf was often added to the top of the lower door to accommodate leaning elbows and packages deposited by itinerant tinkers and traveling merchants.

Today, Dutch doors typically are constructed like a pair of swinging casement windows stacked one on top of the other. The elegant cedar Dutch door shown here is modeled on the appearance of a four-panel, plank Craftsman-style door.

Dining with the backdrop of an arched boulder stone fireplace and honey-toned coffered pine ceiling establishes a warm and intimate feeling throughout the open plan. The kitchen is just 9 ft. 5 in. by 12 ft., but its flush cabinets, monochromatic color scheme, and hidden lighting work together to make it look larger than it is.

The two bedrooms are snuggled under the pitched roof, with operable casement windows located on both gable ends. Skylights provide additional light in the master bedroom. Islands off the coast of Washington have their fair share of gloomy days, and on those occasions a small cottage needs some activity space. The ceiling in the children's room follows the pitch all the way up the gable roof, providing enough height to slip a skylighted loft under the ridge beam.

△ The curve of the fireplace surround complements the stone and contrasts with the overlapping geometries of the exposed-beam ceiling. The top of the mantel, which aligns with the windowsill, implies a unifying horizontal band.

◁ Variation in wood grain, color, and texture is celebrated in these simple Craftsman kitchen cabinets. The beveled drawer and door edges create shadow lines that echo the tone of the dark wood door pulls.

The room is just the right size for stretching out with a board game until the sun shines through the skylight and gives the "okay to play outdoors" signal.

The Clearing

The term *cottage garden* tends to call up images of overplanted gardens with lots of hollyhocks and blousy rosebushes. For many of us, cottage pleasures may include gardening, but more often our gardens are the entire landscape around the cottage, enjoyed for its diversity more than for prize-specimen plants. This cottage has no tame plantings. Instead, it is surrounded on three sides by fir trees, ferns, ground cover, and dappled light. By contrast, the sunny spot of lawn behind the cottage is magical, like a fairy circle discovered in the woods.

△ **The woodwork in the children's bedroom combines usefulness, beauty, and delight. The ladder, with its wood pegs, smooth finish, and rounded ends, is a work of art that carries the kids up to the loft.**

COTTAGE PEDIGREE

LIKE A HOUSE IN PARADISE

The coffered ceiling of this cottage is a microcosm of the cottage itself. The warmth of natural wood, the craft of good building, and the intimacy of well-scaled design have all been blended to create the perfect ceiling and the perfect living space.

Both ceiling and cottage have a structural purpose—the ceiling to hold up the upper floor and the cottage to provide shelter. Both fulfill the function of creating a space for dining, discussion, and work at home. And both glory in the Snow White, cottage-in-the-woods

image that gives this tiny cottage such allure.

The rough-hewn structural wood members of the ceiling conjure up the feeling of sitting beneath the branches of trees. Most likely Adam and Eve lived in an "aedicule," the progenitor of all buildings, a basic hut made of four peeled-bark columns supporting four peeled-bark beams. Like Adam and Eve's house in Paradise, this ceiling expresses the simplicity and strength of the most basic of buildings.

△ The owners tamed a bit of the woodland landscape with a handkerchief patch of lawn that sets the cottage off from the dense woods. A gay perennial border edged with a woven twig picket completes the transition from lawn to paved patio.

◁ The peaked ceiling, open window flaps, and treetop views lend a tentlike feeling to the children's bedroom. Single beds placed toe-to-toe reinforce the camp atmosphere.

Basking in the Sun

Polite exuberance is the leitmotif of John and Sally's elegant warm-weather retreat on the North Carolina island of Bald Head. This graceful, cheerful cottage is a distinctly contemporary interpretation of the late-Gothic Victorian style. Architects Chuck and Anna Dietsche designed the 3,200-sq.-ft., two-story, three-bedroom cottage as a vacation place for the couple, incorporating plenty of room for their adult children to join them on long weekends.

From the doubled-up brackets to the many shingle patterns and plentiful windows, the high-spirited exterior of the twin-gabled cottage is robustly neo-Victorian. With its steeply pitched projecting cross gables, multitextured exterior woodwork, mossy green paint tones, transom windows, porches, and classical columns, the picturesque cottage could be crowned a Folk Victorian or a Queen Anne. Completing the postcard-perfect image of a Victorian cottage, a circular garden planted with colorful ornamental grasses and surrounded by a bright white picket fence introduces the entry.

◁ **The mixing and matching of textures and patterns animates the façade, from top to bottom and side to side. Crimped, wave-pattern shingles lap the two front gables, split shake shingles steady the second story, and smooth, vertical board siding stands upright across the first floor.**

△ The large, second-story gable encloses a screened-in dining room, just off the kitchen. The overhanging gable, supported by two oversized classic columns, provides protective cover over the deep, bowed part of the wraparound porch.

Wooden boardwalks wend their way up to the front porch, which is sheltered from the sun by a Victorian-style arched arbor. But while Victorians shied away from the sunshine, this contemporary Victorian-style cottage also celebrates it. Beaux Soleil—Beautiful Sunshine—is the name Sally and John gave their summer getaway, and they love to bask in the sunlight that bathes the upper porches and living spaces.

Sweet Solitude

One of the hallmarks of cottages is that they are designed for the way the owners want to live; they don't strictly follow convention. At Beaux Soleil, the living rooms are on the second floor and are combined in a hospitable open plan that is modern and genteel. The bedrooms are tucked under the second-floor overhang and encircled by porches that connect to the private backyard. The result is that the bedrooms and sitting rooms are cool and shady, while the living rooms enjoy abundant light and views of the distant water.

The western half of the ground level has two guest bedrooms, with shared bath, to accommodate visiting family or friends. Three window walls make the larger guest room so open and airy that it feels like a sleeping porch. The second

A COTTAGE WITH ITS OWN GLOSSARY

There's a studied exuberance in this cottage, from the wave pattern in the upper-story shingles to the patterned picket fence below.

Bellyband: This swooping decorative trimwork at the base of the upper story began life as a "water table" designed to direct water away from the floor below.

Oval window: Set off with abundant decorative molding, these windows frame the interior view like a magical eye or "oculus."

Arbor: Horizontal battens supported by smooth-shafted 12-in.-diameter columns form an airy shelter that provides sun cover.

Brackets: Originally meant to carry the weight of horizontally projecting building parts, these decorative extensions connect the various exterior and inte-

rior decorative pieces to each other and secure them to the building.

Wave shingle pattern: The gable end extension is given even more definition with this dynamic shingle pattern.

Picket fence: By varying the size and rhythm of the pickets, a simple but distinctive appearance is achieved.

◁ **Crowned by the steeply angled beaded-board ceiling, the kitchen is the focal point of activity. The counters and storage follow the curve of the bow window; complementing the curve is a generous island that borrows colors, details, and materials from the cottage exterior.**

△ The ornately carved bed posters point skyward toward the simple coved ceiling, where a ceiling fan rotates lazily. The spiky tropical plants visible through the porch windows enhance the exotic mood.

guest room opens out to the backyard porch, a portion of which is covered by the projecting dining porch. Two over-sized classical columns that support the dining porch loosely define an outdoor enclosure.

Sally and John's master bedroom is separated from the guest rooms by a small sitting area that offers refreshing views of the shady backyard. The master bedroom has a full bath, walk-in closet, and direct access to a private, screened side porch and the shared back porch. At the eastern edge of the back porch, a seating wall screens views of the master bedroom from the backyard.

A New Perspective

The updated late Victorian imagery of the exterior—textured and patterned walls, carved kingpin trusses, and earthy colors—is continued on the interior, bringing the outside in. Designed for socializing, the second floor is basically an open plan with two alcoves, one for outdoor dining and the other a quiet sitting room. Comfy furniture is grouped

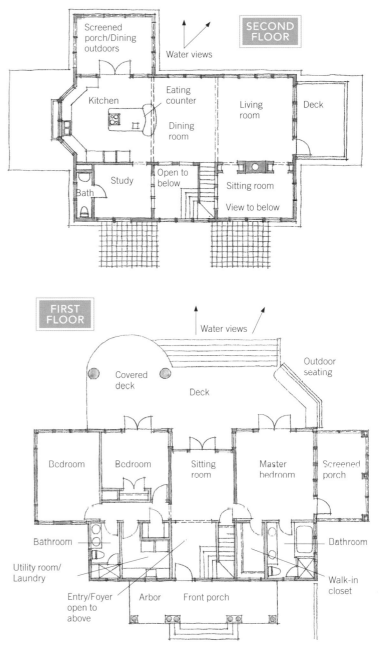

SECOND FLOOR

Screened porch/Dining outdoors

Water views

Kitchen

Eating counter

Living room

Deck

Dining room

Study

Open to below

Bath

Sitting room

View to below

FIRST FLOOR

Water views

Covered deck

Deck

Outdoor seating

Bedroom

Bedroom

Sitting room

Master bedroom

Screened porch

Bathroom

Bathroom

Utility room/ Laundry

Entry/Foyer open to above

Arbor

Front porch

Walk-in closet

◁ In lieu of gutters, the shingles bow out, like a skirt, to divert the rain away from the outdoor living area. The flat capitals topping the columns that frame the doors are a clever contemporary expression of an Ionic column.

▷ The deeply set bull's-eye window in the living room calls attention, inside and out, to the peak of the gable. Variation in ceiling height and shape creates the impression of a defined room within an open plan.

▷ A double-sided wood-burning fireplace cheers large groups in the great room and warms small gatherings in the parlor. Guests get a sneak peak at the parlor through interior windows overlooking the stairway.

casually in front of the large windows that overlook the ebb and flow of the tidal marsh. Out of the whirl of activity, a small sitting room is tucked in an alcove opposite the double fireplace. A gracefully bowed island at the far end of the living room defines the kitchen area.

The kitchen counters wrap around a broad bay window, offering the cooks and their helpers great views. Built-in appliances are nested in the side cupboards, out of the sight line to the bay window. Pendant glass globes and recessed ceiling fixtures highlight the beaded-board and maple kitchen island. The screened-in dining porch, painted a cool mossy green, is just steps away from the kitchen. The eastern balcony off the living room overlooks the wooded landscape and captures views of the early dawn sky.

John and Sally come south to enjoy the warm climate and the lush landscape. Their architects took full advantage of the sun and shadows to create a cottage where the couple can look at life from a new perspective and in a new light. Tall, vaulted beaded-board ceilings heighten the sense that the second-floor living area floats high above the first-floor rooms. Exposed arched trusses soar to the ridge beam, giving the ceilings the look of an origami bird in flight. As the sun moves across the sky, shadows fleetingly dance across the sloped ceiling planes. The plainly ornamented double-hung windows freeze-frame the luminous coastal skyscape.

▽ Interior windows are featured throughout the cottage, linking indoors and out. The second-floor screened porch connects to the kitchen via a bank of glass doors and windows; when they are open, the two spaces flow together as one.

At the Crossroads

◁ **Variety in small details makes the difference between cookie-cutter housing and quaint communities. Here the pickets of the fence and the pickets of the handrail are different in size and scale.**

The San Juan Islands are halfway between Seattle and Vancouver, an idyllic destination where the air is pure, crime is almost unheard of, suburban sprawl is discouraged, and friendly little historic villages abound. Washington State works hard to manage growth on these charming islands while protecting the woods, water, and wildlife that make them so appealing. That balance of values is what makes the area so popular for second homes and is exactly the character architect John M. Campbell had in mind when he designed Cottages at the Crossroads, a retirement community of 10 cottages in the picturesque seaside village of Eastsound.

The colorful, two-bedroom, two-bath cottage condominiums, just 1,000 sq. ft. to 1,200 sq. ft., cluster around a pedestrian-friendly common green space and a community center. Built in the center of the village, they share a 1.4-acre site and, at seven units per acre, match the density of surrounding Eastsound and the cadence of the lively main street.

Common Ground

John's design demonstrates that a compact development within an existing village can be both dense and attractive. Density allows social interaction among residents to be built right into everyday life at Crossroads. The centrally located community center is where all the cottage owners go to collect their mail, exchange greetings, and gather for meetings. Landscaped walkways link the cottages, giving neighbors frequent opportunities for serendipitous meetings on their way to or from the village. Yet each cottage in this dense cluster has a com-

▽ Painting one cottage green and its neighbor red actually makes the relatively small 25-ft.-wide side yard look bigger. The reason? An illusion of greater size is created when complementary colors are placed next to each other.

FIRST
FLOOR

fortable 25-ft. side yard for a garden and patio. The two parking spaces allocated for each unit are located in landscaped parking lots at the north and south ends of the community. The 20-ft.-wide cottages are not overwhelmed by two-car garages, and walking a few steps to the parking lots is another opportunity for exercise and socialization.

Cottages at the Crossroads was designed primarily for retirees, many of whom move here from larger homes. They want to downsize their homes but not their community involvement. The site is directly across the street from the town's senior center. The close grouping of small cottages, each with its own colorful personality, sends out the signal that Crossroads is home to cottage owners who are independent and actively engaged in the community they share. Set around a curving walkway, the cottages form a lively composition with a steady repetition of cottage gables and a strong rhythm of projecting front porches. Together they sound a note of dynamic activity, human and architectural.

A Vibrant Collection of Cottages

The energy of the neighborhood is reflected in the vibrant colors of the painted wood exteriors: yellow ocher, cerulean blue, Tuscan red, and sage green, each accented with a brick

△ To make a distinctive imprint, cottage owners can customize the fireplace detailing and select the woods and finishes for the floors and kitchen cabinets. The variation in glazed tiles gives a handcrafted look to this fireplace while the warm, reddish hue of the Douglas fir makes the mantel an attractive focal point.

Cottages at a Garden Crossroads

{ Inside & Out } The cottages in this community have the best of two worlds. They share a public green space that is representative of the traditional large cottage landscape of old, and each cottage has its own small garden and yard. Great care was taken in the selection of colorful and seasonally distinctive plant material. Over time, the leafy trees will shade porches and parking, yet the common green will remain open and sunny for games and gatherings.

Because the free time and funds of cottage owners may be limited, the individual gardens and yards have been scaled down to provide outdoor space and gardening opportunities that are manageable. Located on the public side of the community picket fence, the miniature garden plots enable everyone to enjoy the efforts of the collective neighborhood. The white wood picket fences that hug the sidewalk are punctuated by arbors or trellises that provide a polite signal that the small yards beyond are private.

◁ The simple interior finishes allow cottage owners to express their own personal style through paint colors and favorite furnishings. Wherever possible, walls are opened up for visibility and a spacious feeling.

TRUSSES IN THE ATTIC

Framing attic lofts and second floors in rafters may create charming living spaces, but it's not necessarily cost effective because of the extra labor and material required. Even intimate cottages such as these can benefit from the efficiency of using inexpensive machine, or gang-nailed, trusses and standard precut 8-ft.-long studs.

The attic baths and bedrooms in these cottages were built with gang-nail trusses. These particular trusses were called upon only to provide the minimal structural support of conventional stud framing, but they added the benefit of economy. Time and money saved using these prefabricated trusses could be spent instead on such handcrafted detailing as the gable sun ornament in the entry dormer, the porch guardrail, the window trim, and even the fireplace mantel.

△ Sunlight floods the dining room and kitchen, highlighting the beaded-board wainscoting. The half wall created by a cutout creates a spacious feel, even though the opening is only slightly wider than a standard doorway.

red door and white window trim and porch rails. A sunburst pattern with gilded address is inset into the gable end of each porch roof. Shingles in variegated shades of gray drape across the roofs like a blanket to unify the collection of cottages, while the vividly painted shed dormers poke through playfully.

The 10 cottage interiors are variations on a simple plan—a first-floor bedroom, bath, living room, dining room, and kitchen, with an extra room and bath under the eaves. In each cottage, the living room has a gas fireplace, the dining room has a wide window seat facing the garden, and the kitchen enjoys a close connection to the dining room, entry, and porch. Each owner selects the interior finishes and decides whether the second-floor space will serve as a guest bedroom, studio, or home office.

Since so many of the owners moved here from larger homes, John came up with simple yet clever ways to make the small, narrow cottages look gracious and spacious. Incorporating lots of windows and generous wall openings was key to capturing light and expansive views of the gardens and the commons. All of the cottages are oriented east and west, so that they soak up daylight all day long. This sunny aspect is a feature that John, who now lives in one of the delightful cottages, enjoys every day from the vantage point of his own home office.

△ Sunburst patterns over entries have long been a cottage favorite. Hefty squared-off brackets, columns, and slim rattail rafters give this entry a bright and welcoming touch.

△ The front porch is an extension of the entry, providing a warm and gracious outdoor place for lingering good-byes or chatting with a passing neighbor. The white square picket rail is a unifying feature for all the cottage porches.

△ Shared public walkways and cottage entry walks are concrete, but the walks in the private side yards are more decorative and personal. Crafted of brick edged with timbers, these walkways have more warmth, texture, color, and visual interest.

Stepping Back in Time

When a San Francisco professional couple told architects Siegel and Strain they wanted to get away from it all, they really meant it. They wanted a weekend cottage where they and their two small children could get away from the city, from formality, from conventional building methods, and even from air-conditioning.

The couple owned a 2½-acre parcel in the arid hills of northern California wine country. Less than a two-hour drive from the city, it was close enough to be easily accessible on weekends. The hillside site blends ancient oak trees and grassy meadowland and enjoys long views to the steep wooded hills beyond. Wineries create a patchwork of green for miles around. Just looking at these pristine surroundings gives the couple the feeling that they have stepped back in time to the 1850s, when sadder-but-wiser Gold Rush miners became farmers in this fertile territory.

The idea of a cottage that would melt into the landscape and work with nature appealed to the couple. Hence the design of the earth-toned, straw-bale cottage. The low 1,200-sq.-ft. cottage is tucked into the base of the wooded

◁ The ocher-colored walls and the shiny underside of the exposed metal roof reflect and bounce the light from the pendant mechanic's lamps, making the cool, open breezeway glow with hospitality late into the evening hours.

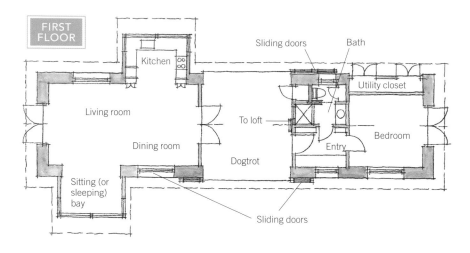

Sliding doors

Bath

Kitchen

Utility closet

Living room

To loft

Bedroom

Dining room

Entry

Dogtrot

Sitting (or sleeping) bay

Sliding doors

hill, where it overlooks the meadow and is shielded from the glare of the western sun. To make the cottage unobtrusive in the landscape and to shelter it beneath the canopy of oaks, the architects created a one-story structure with separate living and bedroom wings. A "dogtrot" breezeway, reminiscent of those the owner remembers from his Tennessee childhood, links the wings. The elemental gable roof and shoebox shape of the cottage pay homage to the simple geometry of century-old agricultural buildings that still dot the local landscape.

Two Halves Make a Whole

The owners describe the straw-bale cottage as "a loaf of bread broken and pulled apart at the dogtrot." The 300-sq.-ft. breezeway acts as a pivot point between the two wings. Traditionally, dogtrots are serene, shaded places for dogs to snooze, but the family dog gets little rest in this active outdoor room, where children scramble up the ladder to the playroom tucked under the roof, cool down in the outdoor shower, or curl up in a deck chair for a bedtime story. The whole family congregates in the dogtrot to enjoy the breezes and tranquil view. Overhead lighting and radiant-heated concrete floors make this outdoor room comfortable and inviting even in the cool of the evening.

STRAW-BALE COTTAGE

Straw has been employed as a construction material for hundreds of years. It was first used in America in the 1890s by pioneers on the Nebraska prairies, where wood was scarce but straw was plentiful. The invention of the baler enabled settlers to build houses from blocks of straw bales that were stuccoed on the exterior and plastered on the interior.

Today, the straw-bale home is enjoying a renaissance around the country, particularly in the Southwest where straw-bale construction builds upon the history, appearance, and popularity of local adobe structures. Straw bales are extremely energy efficient, inexpensive, and easy to build with, and they meet the criteria for green and sustainable building. The three pigs notwithstanding, if constructed properly a straw-bale house can last a century. And from this example, it is easy to see that building with straw bales does not limit creative design possibilities.

△ Gable ends and shed dormers recall vernacular cottages of the area. This cottage adds a new-old twist with straw bale construction of the enclosing walls and fiber cement siding for the projecting sleeping and kitchen bays.

◁ To keep the cottage cool in summer and warm in winter, the architect chose thick interior plaster walls and radiant-heated concrete floors. The heated interior floors are smooth and shiny, a pleasing contrast with the rough concrete exterior floor.

△ The interior cottage walls are clear-finished birch plywood that shimmers in the light. Operable wood casement windows are set deeply into the straw-bale walls for maximum light and minimum glare and heat gain.

△ At the opposite end of the cottage but less than 50 ft. away from the children's sleeping alcove, the parents have their own bedroom wing. It opens wide to a private terrace through double French wood doors for a peaceful view over the meadow to distant forested hills.

Each gable end of the slender cottage opens to an outdoor terrace that burrows into the natural slope of the site. Shaded by an ancient oak and tall fir trees, the light-dappled southern terrace leads into the living wing. Double French doors open the parents' bedroom wing to the northern patio. The view from here to the distant hills extends across the meadow, which has been planted with native plants that thrive even in drought conditions.

The 2-ft.-thick straw-bale walls are excellent insulators, keeping the cottage cool throughout the summer, without air-conditioning, and warm in the winter. The operable windows are set deep into the walls, effectively shading the glass. The slim 25-ft. width of the cottage ensures that cooling breezes and sunlight easily fill the living space.

Inside the House of Straw

Cottage time for this couple is all about being with family. The glow of yellow-painted plaster walls combines with the ocher-stained concrete floors and the clear-finished birch plywood wall and ceiling panels to create a warm, relaxing atmosphere. Red mahogany windows and doors punctuate the earthy color scheme to add some playful zip.

The 15-ft. by 18-ft. living and dining area is the heart of the cottage. Two small alcoves with swooping ceilings extend out from it. The western alcove, close to the action, houses the kitchen. Tall, operable kitchen windows provide excellent ventilation and offer the cook a vista of tangled and gnarly oak branches. The children sleep in the cozy eastern alcove, where they can doze off while their parents linger over dinner a few feet away.

When it's time to retire, the parents cross the breezeway to their Spartan, 15-ft. by 26-ft. bedroom. In the sparingly furnished room, views through large windows and French doors take center stage. The scenic panorama, from neighboring vineyards to the distant hills, fulfills the cottage's promise of an intimate connection with nature.

△ The children drift off to sleep in an alcove just off the living room, lulled by the rhythm of their parents' conversation. Cottage living offers opportunities to enjoy togetherness and build memories that last a lifetime.

△ To preserve the view of the steep, wooded hillside behind the cottage, most of the kitchen storage is below the counter and wide, stacked windows are above. Birch cabinets fitted with minimal hardware complement the understated look of the living rooms.

Up, Up, and Away

When it was built as worker housing in 1922, "Longfellow Creek" was a sparkling, white-shingled 850-sq.-ft. cottage. Modest and unprepossessing, it was indistinguishable from hundreds of other one-story West Seattle cottages. That's no longer the case. The new three-level, 1,025-sq.-ft. addition designed by architect Lisa McNellis turns heads and creates smiles. As colorful and playful as a crayon box, the cottage reaches toward the sky. The reward for climbing to the very top is privacy and a great view of the Seattle skyline.

The cottage is home to the architect, her husband, Grant, and their two children. When they first moved to Seattle, they rented the cottage while looking for a place to buy. A decade later, the owners offered to sell the cottage to Lisa and Grant. The family liked the idea of re-infusing the character of old Seattle with a witty new addition. The lot is small, bounded in back by a steep slope down to Longfellow Creek. To retain any of the backyard, the logical solution was to build a vertical addition alongside the cottage. Wood-shingle facing, decorative siding, and rat-tail rafters are all

◁ The French doors of the home studio open to the shady stone courtyard. The level change from the front entry and the variety of textures and colors of the cottage exterior enhance the sense of the courtyard as an outdoor room.

FIRST FLOOR

Terrace/Deck

Bath

Kitchen

Studio

Dining room

Family/Guest room

Garage

Living room

Porch

△ When the cottage was built in 1922, the Seattle skyline looked nothing like today's view as seen from the third-floor landing. This humble little worker's cottage has grown up with the city.

△ The colorful mustard yellow and beet red of the exterior promise delectable taste on the interior. The varied forms of the addition and the original cottage are as well composed as a tangy tossed salad.

elements found on 1920s worker cottages. The new shingles are oversized, the scalloped siding evolved into board and batten, and the rattail rafters became an arbor over the new entryway.

Something similar to the keystone in an arch was needed to fuse the old and new cottage halves into a whole. Lisa's solution was a 225-sq.-ft. entry arcade that gets a lot of traffic in all different directions. On their way to meet with Lisa in her home office, clients are led through the entry to a small dry-garden courtyard. Guests are welcomed into the original cottage, which houses the living room, dining room, kitchen, and den. Family members can slip up the stairs to the two-story bedroom tower or pass through the laundry/mudroom to the garage.

Lisa's inspiration for the bedroom tower was a tree house, in which each of the bedrooms perches like a bird's nest on a branch. The narrow footprint of the bedroom tower ensures that natural light—a precious commodity in the Pacific Northwest—can flow from the floor-to-ceiling interior window in Lisa and Grant's master bedroom to light

△ Vertical board-and-batten siding mixes it up with horizontal lap-shingle siding to create a fun and dynamic cottage exterior. A curved bench for two takes the place of a porch rail.

△ Little white "buttons" punctuate the spots where the treads meets the risers, adding an upholstered look to the stair. The custom-designed iron handrail accentuates the twists and turns of the stairwell.

▷ Finely scaled metal rungs and handrails that seem to curve around a tree trunk add to the tree house metaphor of this cottage addition. You can circle the "trunk" up to the bird's-nest bedroom, or climb up the ladder to the hideaway.

the hallway. Their son's third-floor rookery bedroom hovers above the two second-floor bedrooms and has a great view of downtown Seattle from the large stairwell window.

Maximize and Minimize

When remodeling, it is easy to get carried away thinking about tearing down walls and rearranging floor plans. But the money spent tearing down each wall might be better spent on high-quality finishes in the new construction. By minimizing structural changes to the original cottage, Lisa and Grant were able to maximize their budget.

△ Seattle gets more rain and overcast skies than any other large U.S. municipality, so light is at a premium even in a multiwindowed tower cottage like this.

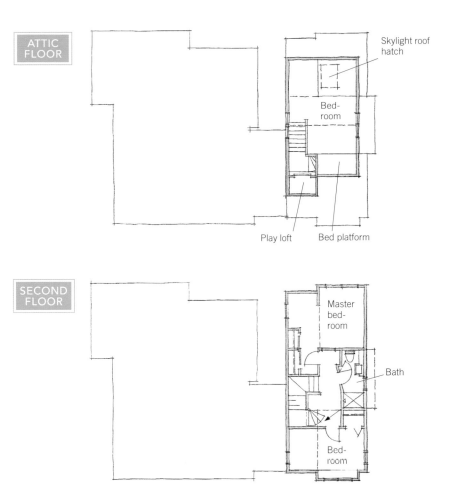

ATTIC FLOOR

Skylight roof hatch

Bed-room

Play loft

Bed platform

SECOND FLOOR

Master bed-room

Bath

Bed-room

AN INDOOR TREE HOUSE

Nooks & Crannies The tall, narrow tower cottage, with its circulation challenges and limited space, presents design problems that the architect has solved with ingenuity and humor. At the very top of the tower, beneath the gabled roofs, she tucked a play loft and an intimate bedroom for the children.

Getting to those rooms is half the fun. What kid wouldn't want to climb a nifty spiral stair or warm wood steps and then a metal ladder on the way to his or her very own play loft? This is a tree house...but inside. The crow's-nest bedroom is also special, so clever in configuration that it doesn't need a door— the serpentine circulation and wall layout allow just the right amount of privacy without one.

The plan of the original cottage worked quite well. The kitchen was the only room that required a major redesign. Lifting the roof and adding a wall of operable windows transformed that tight, dark room into a glowing and open contemporary space. The use of small, 2-in.-sq. wall tiles, delicate pendant lights, and unobtrusive cabinet hardware furthers the illusion of spaciousness. The outdoor dining deck is located conveniently just off the kitchen. It is twice as large as the formal, interior dining room and just as elegant, with wood plank floors and a handrail of horizontal wood and steel cable members.

The cottage is as serene on the interior as it is playful on the exterior. The palette of finish materials—white walls, natural wood trim, simple ironwork, hardwood floors, neutral bedroom carpet, and abundant windows—gives the addition a lighter-than-air quality. Yet the enlarged cottage retains the intimate feeling of the original worker cottage, with a unique nook or cranny for every member of the family.

▷ The sloping roofline of the original Craftsman cottage was lifted to create generous ceiling height in the new kitchen. The owners emphasized the diagonal in the kitchen as a visual memento of their home's history.

△ The focal point of the living room is the hearth, with its wrought-iron grate and Douglas fir and stone mantel. The white walls crisply offset the dark-stained fir floors.

Outdoor Connections

{ Inside & Out } Lisa McNellis has made the most of a site constricted by zoning ordinances, steep topography, existing plant material, and the complexity of adding on to an existing single-story ranch cottage. By weaving together a play of indoor and outdoor spaces, she has created a village of cottage opportunities. The gardenlike outdoor room that serves as the forecourt to her tower cottage is like an arcaded village street. Visitors have the option of entering the domestic wing of the house or continuing on to the at-home office.

On the other side of the site, the wood deck broadens the outdoor options of the "public" or social zone of this cottage by connecting to the kitchen and dining room. Dense plantings combine with the deck to form an outdoor room that is both an extension of the social space within and its own distinct dining or multitasking room outside.

Family Tradition

David grew up summering at his parents' cottage in Bay View, Michigan, surrounded by an extended clan of family members who also owned cottages. He brought his wife, Suzu, up to Bay View for the first time while they were dating. Now that they are married and have two children, they too summer in Bay View, continuing the family tradition and enjoying their skillfully renovated 1888 cottage.

Bay View became a popular destination in 1876, when hundreds of people came by railroad or steamboat for the area's first Methodist Chautauqua assembly. A year later, the Chautauqua tent campground, on a wooded, sloping bank overlooking Little Traverse Bay, had already taken more permanent shape: Streets were laid out, and simple cottages were erected. Today, the 338-acre site is a web of narrow, curving streets bejeweled with more than 400 delightfully ornamented Victorian cottages. Narrow setbacks and a "no fence" rule preserve the neighborly ambiance of the community, which is listed in the National Register of Historic Places.

◁ The living room is a primer in the straightforward construction of uninsulated cottages. Each notched beam sits squarely on an exposed doubled-up stud, and the large windows are framed simply.

▽ Fittingly, old-fashioned plants such as pink gladiola sprays, ribbed hostas, feathery ferns, and a fragrant cedar thicket grace the lawn and stone terrace of the turn-of-the-century cottage. Bright impatiens add a modern touch of color.

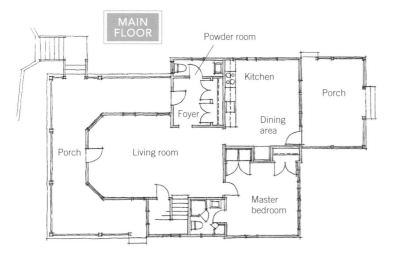

MAIN FLOOR

Powder room · Kitchen · Porch · Foyer · Dining area · Porch · Living room · Master bedroom

Fulfilling a Vision

David and Suzu's two-story cottage looks like one of those lucky finds we all dream about—a period cottage in pristine condition. But when they first peeked in the front door of the 1,900-sq.-ft., four-bedroom, four-bath cottage, they saw a 100-year accumulation of bad remodeling decisions. The entire interior was cloaked in layers of cheap carpet, vinyl flooring, and simulated wood paneling. Not one bit of the original Victorian charm was evident inside. Suzu is an interior designer, and she was fearless in her vision that the true character of the cottage would reveal itself when the decades of "improvements" were peeled away.

Whenever possible during the remodel, Suzu salvaged, restored, refinished, and reused original doors, windows, flooring, and wainscoting. She worked with local architect Rick Neumann and local craftsmen, all of whom had experience remodeling Bay View cottages that enabled them to meet the high standards required by the community's architectural review board and mandated by the National Register.

▷ Steamboat Gothic gingerbread scrollwork like that on the front screen door whimsically embellishes the 1880s cottages of Bay View. Other decorative sawn-wood porch details, from the flat and angular column capitols to the balustrades and sawtooth dentils, punctuate the porch like exclamation points.

△ New windows in the remodeled master bedroom were framed with doubled-up, grooved 1x4s. Over the iron bed, two inward-swinging 2 over 2 casement windows provide maximum ventilation.

STAIR MOVES

{Nooks & Crannies} Relocating the stair from the center of the living room to a position against the wall made the living room of this cottage larger and more cohesive. The new stair provides a more direct route to the bedrooms above but matches the spirit of the original cottage in construction and appearance. Antique leaded windows that were found lying under the porch have been installed above the winder landing, where they contribute warmth and daylight to the stairs and both floors.

▷ A classic cast-iron claw-foot tub is tucked under the sloping eaves. The narrow rectangular shower enclosure and slender, arching shower nozzle highlight the room's intimate scale, as does the miniature square window.

An awkwardly located stairway blocked windows, keeping sunlight from penetrating into the living room. David wanted to brighten the space and make it more inviting for large gatherings. Suzu came up with the idea of relocating the stair to the wall opposite the entry foyer, thus creating one large, light living room. She also merged three small rooms on the first floor to fashion a master bedroom suite. Most of the family meals take place in the generous-sized 14-ft. by 16-ft. kitchen or out on the wraparound porch.

At one point, the cottage was a boarding house, which explains why each of the three bedrooms on the second floor had its own bathroom. Suzu updated the bathrooms with new plumbing and wiring while retaining the simplicity of 19th-century bathrooms.

All the interior exposed wood walls and ceilings are painted a creamy white, while the floors and door trim are

△ Even more ornate than the decorative exterior woodwork, the antique sink in this small, beaded-board bathroom, with its original marble vanity, curlicue cast-iron support, and rosette decoration, creates an authentic Victorian atmosphere.

▽ Mixed and matched antique chairs set a traditional yet informal tone for the big eat-in kitchen, which also includes an old-fashioned-style deep porcelain sink and extra-long crookneck faucet. A touch of Steamboat Gothic ornamentation shows up in the cupboard bracket.

soft olive green. On the exterior, the windows are trimmed in olive and white, and the gingerbread trim is bright, shiny white. The unified palette reinforces the uninterrupted flow from inside to outside that is part and parcel of the cottage experience.

From the Ground Up

By covenant, Bay View cottages can be occupied only between May and October, and the original cottages were simple, inexpensive, uninsulated summer homes, built with little concern for permanence. In fact, David and Suzu discovered that the only things holding up their cottage were some rotting tree stumps. Constructing footings and a partial basement made the cottage structurally sound and also provided space for a new furnace and water heater.

The ornamented, wraparound porches of the cottage are a glorious example of the Steamboat Gothic style. Unfortunately, they were rotten and needed to be rebuilt. Carefully restored to its original splendor, the hospitable first-floor porch hosts gatherings with friends and neighbors. The second-floor porch is a favorite place for quiet times with close family. On hot summer nights it can be called in to duty as a sleeping porch, just as it was more than 100 years ago.

△ **Double-decker verandas, a hallmark of the Steamboat Gothic style, decorate many Bay View cottages. They're named after the steamboats whose decks they resemble; such steamboats brought many families to summer here in the 1900s.**

◁ **Rising up from the hill like a two-tiered wedding cake, the cottage opens to the view with porches that wrap around the first-floor living area and the second-floor bedrooms. The gable peak is ornamented with original sawn-wood scrollwork commemorating the cottage's construction date.**

Hallmark Veranda

{ Inside & Out } If a little veranda is a good thing, then the large porches on this cottage are a very good thing. Wrapping around the cottage on three sides and on two stories, the porches exemplify the benefits of the veranda as a cottage hallmark. Verandas extend the visual and environmental reach of the spaces within, while creating summer's best outdoor rooms. Protected from summer rains, they provide views, breezes, and relaxation under the permanent roof cover. By its very location, the first-floor veranda provides a transition from the public realm of the sidewalk to the private inner keep. What better place for a summer eve's informal visit with neighbors?

True to its Victorian heritage, the first-floor veranda is embellished with an abundance of gingerbread scrollwork. Decorative trim further defines the handrail and eaves line, lending a happy face to this cottage façade.

Deciphering the Past

When Joe Levine set out to transform a pre—Civil War barn into a weekend cottage for his family of four, he knew he was tackling an American icon. Joe is a partner in Bone Levine Architects, a firm that enjoys the respect of preservationists for its great success in breathing new life into old buildings. Whatever the project, Joe enjoys the challenge of deciphering the layers of a building, structural and cultural, to find its spirit.

He and Jane were captivated by the 1,200-sq.-ft. barn on their first visit, when the sun illuminated the entire interior expanse. Capitalizing on this volume and light was obviously going to be important in the renovation. Because the couple was converting the rural Pennsylvania structure into a family cottage, warm living space was also important to them, taking precedence over strict historical accuracy.

The raw materials—weathered wood siding, local fieldstone, and rough-hewn interior posts and beams—had the rich patina that only time can produce. However, there was no doubt that age had taken its toll on the structure. Joe would have to draw on his construction experience and the

◁ The owner wanted to showcase the beauty of simple structure. At night, the hierarchy of columns, beams, and rafters is clearly visible in the illuminated cottage interior, manifesting a virtual lesson in barn construction.

▷ Barn red is an appropriate color for the front door of this pre–Civil War barn transformed into a family cottage. Barn wood siding, the standing-seam metal roof, and a metal-grate "cow catcher" step also reflect the cottage's agricultural heritage.

help of engineers to disassemble the barn completely, build an extended stone foundation, and reassemble the "new" barn.

Following Tradition

The open-plan, twin-lofted, one-bath cottage is a mix of rustic tradition and high tech. To the visitor, it might at first seem more like a New York loft than a 19th-century barn building on the banks of the Delaware River. Yet the steel tension cables and I-beams, the metal spiral stair, and the glass and fiberglass window walls all express current technology, something barn builders have always embraced.

Joe is an excellent craftsman, but he didn't have the time to do the work himself. Luckily, their neighbor is an equally skilled craftsman, and he built all the doors and windows to Joe's high standards. The wood shutters were built from original barn siding, and local fieldstone was used for the new and expanded foundation and the patio. The cherry

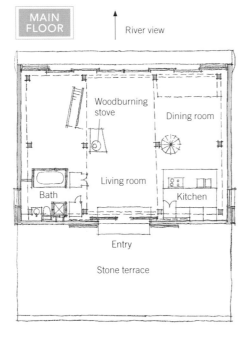

MAIN FLOOR

↑ River view

Woodburning stove

Dining room

Living room

Bath

Kitchen

Entry

Stone terrace

▷ Theater-in-the-round is one way to describe the cottage interior, with its implied rather than explicit walls and simultaneously visible upper and lower levels. Dramatically, yet modestly, a shoji screen "lantern" houses the cottage's only bathroom.

△ Good design is both timely and timeless. The dining room combines 19th-, 20th-, and 21st-century construction technology and furniture design, from Arne Jacobson chairs to antique light fixtures; together and separately they appeal to the senses of touch, sight, and sound.

△ Architects often discourage clients from adding window treatments, usually because there's a beautiful view. Patterned after sliding barn doors, large glass panels on red frames slide across a steel structure; with each adjustment, the views are framed in a new way.

▷ The family brought a preference for spareness to the countryside. Limiting bedroom storage to two wall-hung clothing cupboards keeps wardrobe choices to a minimum. Steel cables stretched across the sleeping platform call attention to the dramatic drop-off.

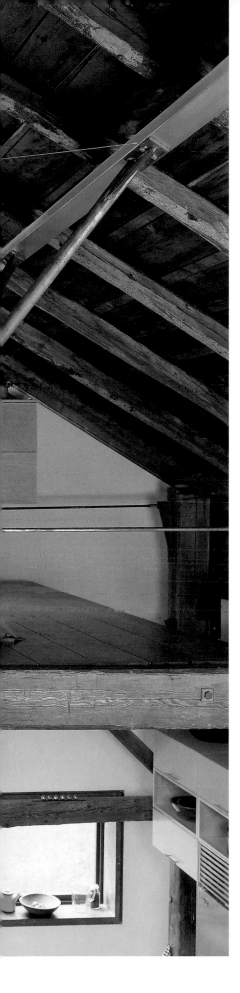

BARN ROOTS

The barn has long served, through influence or adaptation, as a cottage precedent. Because of its utility and pervasive style, this Pennsylvania barn exemplifies its Dutch barn antecedents.

The Dutch settlers of the Schoharie, Mohawk, and Hudson valleys of New York built the first great barns in the United States. Variations on their examples are seen across much of the Northeast to the Midwest. These barns have expansive gable roofs and are often "banked," like this example, by being set into grade at their second level to ease the delivery and distribution of feed to livestock in the level below. The horizontal barn siding of this barn is characteristic of the East, whereas in the Midwest, barn siding typically is vertical.

Windows and openings are kept to a minimum in barns, but where they occur it's as easy to make them large as small, so they usually are large.

Detailing can be simple or less so. Before Mies van der Rohe, there probably was a Dutch barn builder who exclaimed that less is more. Dutch barns often appear much larger than they really are because of their massiveness and simplicity. The hidden beauty of these barns is the substantial yet straightforward structural system in which members are oversized by today's calculation. Beams are mortised, tenoned, and pegged with the ends of cross beams in an easy and elegant manner. The cross beams sometimes project through timber columns that are curved to shape distinctive Dutch barn "tongues."

floors and maple veneer cabinets were designed to complement the weathered wood.

Barn roofs are landmarks in the area. The material on the new cottage roof is standing-seam, lead-coated copper sheeting, a traditional barn roofing material. Joe vented the ridge beam, borrowing common-sense barn ventilation construction. Typically, barnyard landscapes are spare; the stone entry patio sets the cottage apart from the landscape, just as a barnyard sets a barn apart from the farmyard.

Were You Raised in a Barn?

Living in a renovated barn poses privacy and acoustical challenges similar to those experienced in a loft. Because this barn is intended as a weekend cottage where space is intentionally intimate, family members are more tolerant of close

quarters than they might be in a full-time residence. The parents and kids sleep in lofts at opposite ends of the cottage. Each loft is accessed by its own distinctive metal stair. Although privacy is largely psychological, curtains can be drawn. For ultimate privacy, the couple decided to build a one-bedroom, one-bath silo-style guest cottage. Joe and Jane stay in it when their daughters have overnight guests.

The interior of the cottage resembles a minimalist set design. Walls implied by the original posts and beams create zones for the kitchen, dining, and living rooms. The undersides of the loft floors act as lowered ceilings, without shattering the illusion of the cottage as one large interior space. A freestanding wood-burning stove creates a hearth at the entry.

Barns have very few windows. Joe recognized that controlling the number, placement, and size of windows was critical to retaining the spirit of the barn. The windows in the gable ends of the sleeping loft are simply punched out of the clapboard siding, like hayloft doors. Diamond-shaped windows tucked under the eaves are another typical barn hallmark. The glass window wall on the eastern side of the cottage opens to the landscape when the wood shutters are rolled open. When they are rolled shut, the exterior of the cottage recalls the old wooden barn. The shutter boards are spaced with gaps between them to ensure that light filters through exactly as it did when Jane and Joe first peeked into the decrepit barn and saw a diamond in the rough.

A Japanese Puzzle Box

{ Inside & Out } About the time this 19th-century barn was built, the traditional Japanese puzzle box called Himitsu-Bako was being developed in the Hakone region of Japan. Like this cottage, the puzzle consists of well-crafted wooden panels that fit together superbly and can glide apart to reveal a treasure within. Our own puzzle box measures 4 "suns" (4.6 in. x 3.2 in. x 2.25 in.) and requires four moves to reveal the 1887 silver dollars stored inside.

This cottage is a bit larger, more complex, and frames a more significant treasure. It is a full-scale puzzle box equipped with American "shoji" screen wooden shutters and sliding glass windows. Unlike the Japanese puzzle, the cottage can be played with in a variety of ways. Yet much like the puzzle, the treasure and the challenge of play is really the interaction of the indoor and the outdoor. Myriad vistas and views from within this cottage can be created with the many combinations of openings.

△ The well-styled and super-efficient Scandinavian stove radiates heat long after the last embers fade; the metal floor plate is a required noncombustible surround. A beam is pressed into action as a rack for fireplace tools.

△ Sleek maple veneer cabinets and shimmering stainless steel set the kitchen apart from the rough structure. The stainless-steel island with cooktop incorporates electrical outlets around the edges; under-counter storage includes a wine cubby handily sandwiched between the drawers.

△ Sliding wood shutters control light and privacy on the lower level, and curtains do so above. The shutters have gaps so that slivers of light can slip through, recalling the feeling, mood, and look of a working barn suffused with filtered daylight.

All Grown Up

When Nancy and Garry Leonard moved to Connecticut from the Midwest and went house hunting, budget was high on their list of criteria. They found a 1923 English-style summer cottage set back from the main road. Although it was small, and priced accordingly, it sat on a lot large enough to accommodate future additions. As soon as they saw the stone fireplace, the 16-over-16 divided light windows, and the wide-plank pine floors in the living room, they knew this seasonal cottage had the potential to grow with them as their family grew.

Garry is an architect, and it wasn't long before he began designing the first of several phased renovation projects to convert the small vacation cottage into a year-round home. No matter how large or small the project, Nancy and Garry made sure the charm of the original cottage remained.

◁ Beatrix Potter may well have inspired this cottage garden. The hanging shades seen behind the 16-over-16 windows of the gable end lend the look of twinkling eyes watching over the garden for hungry rabbits.

ONE COTTAGE, MANY ROOFS

This cottage has blossomed through five additions and remodelings, with at least two more in the planning stages. It takes a deft touch and a discerning eye to weave together all those growth spurts into one pleasing and cohesive whole. Keeping a coherent- or consistent-looking roof is one of the greatest challenges in the remodeling and addition process. Continuing the same roof pitch throughout, while the easiest way to go, often won't yield the ceiling clearances, the volumes, or even the romance, visual interest, and spatial character that an addition demands.

Architect Garry Leonard has been able to carry off a challenging task here by tying the different roof elements, wall extensions, and new windows together with consistent siding, trim, and roofing material. And, magically, he has made the different roof pitches align.

▷ Typically cottages in this village have fireplaces built with stones gathered from the beach just down the lane. All the neighbors agree this floor-to-ceiling stone fireplace is the grandest of the bunch. Mementos from family trips are displayed in the arched alcoves below the abundant wall-to-ceiling bookcases.

◁ From the front, the 1923 English cottage looks remarkably as it did when it was first built. The new additions were made to the rear and designed to ensure that all the charm and scale of the original wood-shingle gabled cottage were retained.

Holding Fast While Letting Go

The first few renovation projects took place within the existing footprint of the 2,300-sq.-ft. cottage, when Garry moved walls to reconfigure the upper hall into a playroom and the two children's bedrooms. A dormer and skylights now pierce the roof, adding light and headroom for those rooms. Next, Garry added almost 1,000 sq. ft. to the back of the cottage in the form of a two-story turret. The five-sided tower, a romantic structure that contrasts with the gable ends and befits the fairy-tale image of an English cottage, encompasses a new kitchen and breakfast room on the first floor and a master bedroom suite upstairs.

"To match existing" is an oft-repeated note on Garry's architectural drawings, leaving no doubt that the addition would embellish the cottage, not detract from its English style. Since the addition is not visible from the road, some owners might be tempted to use siding rather than wood shingles to match the existing. But Garry and Nancy designed the addition to meet their own standards. No concessions concerning cottage character or quality were allowed inside or out. Yet practicality prevailed when availability became an issue. Instead of 16-over-16 true divided lights like the original cottage windows, for example, the new windows are 8 over 8.

△ The large hallway at the top of the stair used to be the children's playroom; now it serves as a home office. The windowed sage-green alcove grants safe haven to well-loved toys under the gable peak of the front entry.

Most of the cottage woodwork and walls are white to highlight the couple's collectibles. In the dining room, the focus is on the people; the sparsely ornamented, creamy butternut yellow walls and soft gray-green woodwork enhance the atmosphere of friendship and conversation.

The Art of Display

Garry is a senior design associate in the architectural firm of Kevin Roche and John Dinkeloo. His knowledge of display and lighting design shines through in the cottage kitchen. Low-voltage lights beneath the cabinets bathe the counter with a soft glow, and warm, recessed spotlights showcase the china and stainless that are displayed behind glass-fronted cabinet doors.

Garry and Nancy are not only serious cooks but also gracious hosts, and their kitchen gets a real workout. The workspace is open at both ends in a "Pullman" configuration, allowing them to serve their guests conveniently wherever they are—in the living, dining, or breakfast room. The floor-to-ceiling, bleached wood cabinetry provides generous storage in the compact kitchen and adds a sense of quiet elegance to the space.

Creating a feeling of openness and separation of function is accomplished simply by accentuating the transition from one room to the other. The breakfast room is down one step from the kitchen, and an overhead beam demarcates the entry foyer.

The Art of Repose

Nancy works with words all day and Garry with images, so they wanted their bedroom to be a place for simple repose. The only furnishings in the bedroom are the double bed and end tables. Nancy remembers waking up the first morning in her new bedroom. The room was filled with light from the bay window, and the shadow patterns on the fan-shaped ceiling delighted her so much that she declared she was never leaving the bed.

Clothes and shoes are neatly stored in 6-ft.-high closets in the skylight-lit dressing room. Pocket doors save space in the dressing area, but no elegance was sacrificed for efficiency; Garry designed the doors to match the original five-panel doors of the house.

One of the joys of cottage designs is that they are quirky. Garry wanted to celebrate the varying roof pitches on the interior of this cottage. Each room has a different feel, because each ceiling is different. The fan-shaped bedroom ceiling is low and sheltering, the dressing room ceiling extends all the way up to the ridgeline, and a sloping ceiling in the bathroom enhances the intimacy of the room.

Now that the children have grown up, the charming little summer cottage has grown up as well. Garry and Nancy are dreaming about their next project—transforming the garage into an art and architecture studio.

△ Trading spaces, a former bedroom is now a skylit dressing room that doubles as the entry to the master suite. The paneled closet doors and hardwood floors make this an elegant walk-in dressing room.

▷ Garry added visual punch by exploiting drywall's sculptural possibilities. The bedroom ceiling extends all the way to the peak, creating the look of a folded fan, while the carved oculus borrows light and brings sky views into the dressing room.

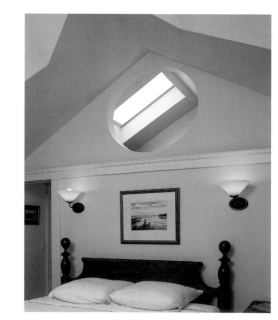

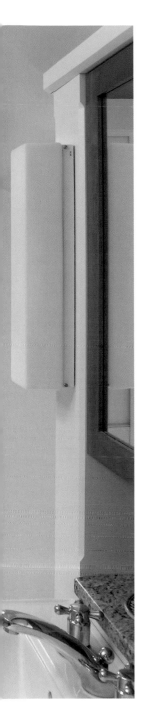

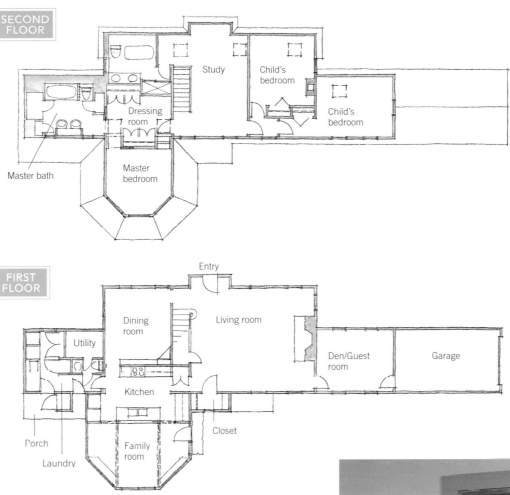

SECOND FLOOR

Master bath

Dressing room

Master bedroom

Study

Child's bedroom

Child's bedroom

FIRST FLOOR

Entry

Dining room

Utility

Living room

Kitchen

Den/Guest room

Garage

Porch

Laundry

Family room

Closet

IN THE CLOSET

{*Nooks &*}
{*Crannies*} When the owners planned one of the first of the many renovations and additions to their cottage, they knew they would be covering up the access to their living room crawlspace. Alternative access in an exposed area was needed.

They solved the problem with creativity and style. A cocoa mat is cut into the floor of the remodeled coat closet and affixed to a removable hatch that covers an opening to the crawlspace. The mat is recessed to define its territory, and its bristle-brush texture helps clean footwear. Practical and well thought out, the mat/cover looks like it belongs there—and it does!

Agora Architects and Planners
Principal Architect: John M. Campbell
P.O. Box 250
Orcas, WA 98280
(360) 376-2035
pp. 158–163

Bauer Askew Architecture
Principal Architect: Tom Bauer
209 10th Avenue
South Suite 407
Nashville, TN 37203
(615) 726-0047
www.bauerarchitecture.com
pp. 36–43

Bone/Levine Architects
Principal Architect: Joe Levine
561 Broadway, Studio 8D
New York, NY 10012
(212) 219-1038
www.bonelevine.net
Contractor: Larry Braverman,
Beach Lake, PA
pp. 186–193

Robert Bruce Architect
Principal Architect: Robert Bruce
1206 Kenbrook Hills Drive
Upper Arlington, OH 43220-4967
(614) 326-0461
pp. 28–35

Ross Chapin Architects
Principal Architect: Ross Chapin
P.O. Box 230
195 Second Street
Langley, WA 98260
(360) 221-2373
www.rosschapin.com
Contractor: Kim Hoelting
Northwest Woods
3631 Woodland Hall Lane
Clinton, WA 98236
pp. 20–27, 142–149

Dietsche + Dietsche Architect
Project Team: Chuck and Anna Dietsche
210 North 15th Street
Wilmington, NC 28401
(910) 251-8340
www.DietscheDietsche.com
pp. 92–99, 150–157

Geise Architects
Project Architect: Judy Tucker
81 Vine Street, Suite 202
Seattle, WA 98121
(206) 441-1440
www.geise.net
pp. 120–125

Historical Concepts
Design Team: James Strickland,
Terry Pylant, and Zhi Feng
430 Prime Point, Suite 103
Peachtree City, GA 30269
(770) 487-8041
www.historicalconcepts.com
pp. 44–51 , 68–75

Garry Leonard, Architect
63 Neck Road
Madison, CT 06443
pp. 194–201

Robert Luchetti Associates
Project Team: Robert Luchetti,
Noel Clarke, and Donna Ficca
14 Arrow Street
Cambridge, MA 02138
(617) 492-6611
www.luchetti.com
pp. 60–67

Mackey Mitchell Associates
Design Team: Gene Mackey, John
Guenther, and Paul Weunnenberg
800 Saint Louis Union Station, Suite 200
Saint Louis, MO 63103
(314) 421-1815
www.mackeymitchell.com
pp. 112–119

McNelis Architects
Principal Architect: Lisa McNelis
4218 SW Alaska Street
Seattle, WA 98116
(206) 938-4086
www.mcnelisarchitects.com
pp. 170–177

Mosaic Design Studio
Designer: Lisa Cini
879 North High Street
Columbus, OH 43215
(614) 429-6800
www.mosaicdesignstudio.com
pp. 100–105

Richard Neumann, Architect
604 Bay Street
Petoskey, MI 49770
(231) 347-0931
Interior Designer: Suzu Neithercut
pp. 178–185

Robert Orr & Associates
441 Chapel Street
New Haven, CT 06511
(203) 777-3387
www.robertorr.com
pp. 134–141

Robert Page, Architect
162 Montowese Street
Branford, CT 06405
(203) 481-2555
pp. 106–111

Siegel & Strain Architects
Design Team: Henry Siegel and
Larry Strain
1296 59th Street
Emoryville, CA 94608
(510) 547-8092
www.siegelstrain.com
pp. 164–169

Vetter Denk Architects
Project Architect: Brian Filkins
614 North Broadway
Milwaukee, WI 53202
(414) 223-3388
www.vetterdenk.com
pp. 76–83

Rob Whitten Architects
P.O. Box 404
37 Silver Street
Portland, ME 04112
(207) 774-0111
pp. 126–133

A. Richard Williams, Architect, FAIA
Pointe La Barbe Road
St. Ignace, MI 49781
pp. 52–59